The Spiritual Writings of Amir ᶜAbd al-Kader

SUNY Series in Western Esoteric Traditions
David Appelbaum, Editor

The Spiritual Writings of Amir ʿAbd al-Kader

Michel Chodkiewicz

Translated by a team under the direction of
James Chrestensen and Tom Manning

State University of New York Press

Originally published in France
under the title *Écrits Spirituels*

English translation made by agreement with Editions du Seuil

Published by
State University of New York Press, Albany

Printed in the United States of America

For information, address State University of New York Press, State University Plaza, Albany, N.Y., 12246

Production by Diane Ganeles
Marketing by Bernadette LaManna

Library of Congress Cataloging-in-Publication Data
ʿAbd al-Qādir ibn Muḥyī al-Dīn, Amir of Mascara, 1807?–1883.
[Mawāqif. English]
The spiritual writings of Amir ʿAbd al-Kader/Michel Chodkiewicz ; translated by a team under the direction of James Chrestensen and Tom Manning.
p. cm. — (SUNY series in Western esoteric traditions)
Includes index.
ISBN 0-7914-2445-6 (alk. Paper).—ISBN 0-7914-2446-4 (pbk. : alk. paper)
1. Islam—Doctrines. I. Chodkiewicz, Michel. II. Chrestensen, James. III. Manning, Tom. IV. Title. V. Series.
BP166.A232713 1995
297'.2—dc20 94-28385
CIP

10 9 8 7 6 5 4 3 2 1

إهداء

إلى روح المرشد الكامل

الوارث الأكبر العارف بالله

الشيخ مصطفى عبد العزيز .

Contents

Introduction

Just as there is no place where God is not, there is no state where saintliness cannot find a place. Whether anchorites or wanderers, princes who retreat to the desert, merchants who abandon their shops and go begging by the roadside, there is in Islam no lack of vocations which take their impulse from renunciation and find their fulfillment in exile. But perfection does not come from these ruptures. The best stay where they are, since "He is with you wherever you are" (Kor. 57:4).[1] They do not flee their condition, be they caliph or water bearer; sometimes it is their condition which flees them. Their retreat is the crowd, their desert is the public square. Conformity is their asceticism, the ordinary is their miracle. The lesser holy war against the enemy outside does not divert them from the greater holy war against the infidel which everyone carries in himself. Neither does the greater holy war divert them from the lesser. Their lives unite the affairs of worldly life and those of eternity without regret, if not without effort. They are like that "excellent tree" spoken of in the Koran (14:24) "whose root is firm and whose branches are in heaven," symbol of the *axis mundi,* that is to say "the perfect man" (*al-insān al-kāmil*) who, by virtue of the divine mandate (*khilāfa*), unites in his person the higher realities and the lower realities (*al-ḥaqaʾiq al-ḥaqqiyya wa al-khalqiyya*).

This saintliness does not wear a uniform or carry an emblem. A brilliant destiny can disguise it as easily as an obscure life. The destiny of ʿAbd al-Kader made one forget that he was anything other than (indeed much more than) a magnanimous swordsman, or, as Bugeaud said "a man of genius whom history should place alongside of Jugurtha."[1bis] But Bugeaud probably suspected that the amir was not only that. On May 30, 1837, for the first and, it would appear, the last time, he met ᶜAbd al-Kader. The treaty of Tafna had been signed the day before. It was accompanied by a secret agreement containing concessions which Bugeaud did not have the authority to grant. Everyone was deceived: first of all France, because the general had committed it beyond his instructions, but especially the amir, who had been misled by the ambiguous wording of the text concerning the true intentions of an adversary he had believed trustworthy. The only interests which were well taken care of in this affair were those of Bugeaud himself. Quite shamelessly, the general had obtained from the amir a commission of one hundred and eighty thousand francs "to guarantee the maintenance of the local roads in his jurisdiction"—he was also deputy of Dordogne—and his consent to some generous payments to Bugeaud's officers. In the end Bugeaud gave back the money, since this strange bargain caused a stir. In 1838 a trial revealed to the French public that this example of extortion was not unique and that Bugeaud had other irons in the fire. None of this, however, would prevent Bugeaud from becoming Governor-General of Algeria in 1840 and Maréchal in 1843.[2]

The day after his meeting with ᶜAbd al-Kader, Bugeaud described the amir in a letter to Count Molé, president of the Conseil: "He is pale and somewhat resembles the way that Jesus Christ is often portrayed."[3] This strong impression was not produced solely by the physical appearance of the person. Bugeaud recognized in the amir a grandeur of an order which transcended the categories of a soldier and tried to define it in a letter on January 1, 1846: "He is a kind of prophet, the hope of all fervent Muslims."[4]

Bugeaud was a fairly dense scoundrel. Léon Roche was of a more ductile metal. Pretending to convert to Islam, he became close to the amir and secretly served the French interests until the day when, his treason proven, he fled after a scene during which ᶜAbd al-Kader showed more sadness and scorn than anger.[5] The memoirs of Roche are far from being as trustworthy on many points as was once thought,[6] but his observations concerning the person of the amir, his character, and his way of life, which are confirmed elsewhere by numerous testimonies, do merit belief. Going beyond the summary remarks of a Bugeaud, they cast some light on the hidden face of ᶜAbd al-Kader. "Where time permits," Roche wrote,[7] "ᶜAbd al-Kader prays outside of his tent at a site cleared for that purpose—and those who wish to participate in the communal prayer, which is the most pleasing to God, place themselves behind him.

"These men, with full and majestic attire, arranged in several lines, at certain intervals repeat in a deep voice the response, God is great! There is no God but God! Mohammed is the prophet of God! They prostrate themselves all together, touch the earth with their foreheads and raise their arms toward heaven as they rise, while the amir recites verses from the Koran. All together, this presents a moving and solemn spectacle.

"The religious exercises of ᶜAbd al-Kader are not limited to this. He gives himself up to meditation between each prayer, constantly touching his prayer beads. Every day, in his tent, or at the mosque when by chance he finds himself in a town, he gives a talk on the unity of God. He is considered one of the most erudite theologians of the time.

"He fasts at least one time a week, and what a fast! From two hours before dawn until sunset, he does not eat, drink, or even inhale any perfume. I don't know if I have mentioned that he rejects the use of smoking tobacco and barely tolerates snuff.

"He rarely allows himself the pleasures of coffee. The moment he sees that it is becoming a habit, he deprives himself of coffee for several days."

This image of a pious and austere warrior is not commonplace. One could hardly imagine Bugeaud reciting his rosary between two calvary charges or commenting on Meister Eckhart around the fires of the bivouac. But neither is this image without precedent. The following episode, which took place during the siege of ᶜAyn Māḍī in 1838 is even more surprising:

"I succeeded with difficulty in getting out of the morass of mud, tombstones, and corpses and I arrived at the tent of ᶜAbd al-Kader in a wretched state. My *bernous* and my *haik* were filthy. In a few words I explained what had just happened to me. ᶜAbd al-Kader had other clothes brought to me and I came and sat next to him. I was under the influence of a nervous excitement which I was unable to master. 'Heal me,' I said to him, 'heal me or I would rather die, for in this state I feel myself incapable of serving you.'

"He calmed me and had me drink an infusion of *schiehh* (a kind of absynthe common in the desert). He supported my head, which I could no longer hold up, on one of his knees. He was squatting in the Arab fashion. I was stretched out at his side. He placed his hands on my head, from which he had removed the *haik* and the *chechias,* and under this gentle touch I soon fell asleep. I awoke well into the night. I opened my eyes and felt revived. The smoky wick of an Arab lamp barely lit the vast tent of the amir. He was standing three steps away from me. He thought I was asleep. His two arms were raised to the height of his head, fully displaying his milky white *bernous* and *haik* which fell in superb folds. His beautiful blue eyes, lined with black lashes, were raised. His lips, slightly open, seemed to be still reciting a prayer but nevertheless were motionless. He had come to an ecstatic state. His aspirations toward heaven were such that he seemed no longer to touch the earth. I had on occasion been granted the honor of sleeping in ᶜAbd al-Kader's tent and I had seen him in prayer and been struck by his mystical transports, but on this night he represented for me the most striking image of faith. Thus the great saints of Christianity must have prayed."[8]

On May 25, 1830, the fleet of Admiral Duperre left Toulon. The conquest began. Fifty-three years later, to the day, ᶜAbd al-Kader died in Damascus. Out of this long half-century, only fifteen years—from 1832 to 1847—would be devoted to combat and the conduct of affairs. Then came the time of exile. ᶜAbd al-Kader surrendered on December 23, 1847. Lamoriciere had promised that he would be allowed to leave for the East. The Duke d'Aumale confirmed this promise. In spite of this the amir was imprisoned, first at Toulon, then at Pau, finally at Amboise until 1852.

Freed by Louis Napoleon Bonaparte, ᶜAbd al-Kader embarked for Istanbul, arriving on January 7, 1853. After a short stay there, he lived in Bursa for two years. In 1856, he took up permanent residence in Damascus. With the exception of several episodes—the protection accorded the Christians endangered by the Druze's revolt in 1860 and the amir's presence at the inauguration of the Suez canal in 1862—this period of his life does not interest historians.[9] They limit themselves to noting the place that devotions had in his life from then on. As we have seen, this is not a question of a belated vocation of a hero retired from the battlefield and we will see that "devotion" is a rather feeble word. But before going further let us cite another testimony by a European observer who, unlike many others, was not exclusively interested in the public man. Here is how the Englishman, Charles-Henry Churchill, who lived in Damascus during the winter of 1859–1860, described the amir's day:

"He awakes two hours before dawn and devotes himself to prayer and religious meditation until sunrise. Then he goes to the mosque. After having spent a half-hour in public devotion, he returns home, has a brief meal and then works in his library until noon. The call of the muezzin invites him once more to the mosque, where his class is already assembled, awaiting his arrival. He takes a seat and opens the book chosen as the basis for discussion. He reads aloud and is constantly interrupted by requests for explanation to which he responds by revealing the many treasures accumulated by means of laborious studies, investigations and research, in the course of his tumultuous life. The session lasts three hours.

"After the afternoon prayer ᶜAbd al-Kader again returns home and spends an hour with his children—his eight sons—examining the progress that they have made in their studies. After that he dines. At sunset he is once again at the mosque, where he instructs his class for an hour and a half. His task as a teacher is now completed for the day.

He still has two hours before him which he spends in his library. After that he retires."[9bis]

Let us decipher these facts of ᶜAbd al-Kader's life. The key is provided by two events which enclose the period in Damascus. The first event is related in the *Tuḥfat al-Zāʾir*, the biography of the amir by his son Mohammed.[10] ᶜAbd al-Kader left Bursa on the fifth of the month of *rabi al-thani*, 1272 A.H. (1855 A.D.), accompanied by some hundred people. As he neared Damascus, a long procession of dignitaries came out to meet him. But his first visit was not to these notables. Followed by this somewhat disconcerted official escort, he went first of all the tomb of Ibn ᶜArabī, "the greatest spiritual master" (*al-shaikh al-akbar*). Ibn ᶜArabī, who was born in Andalusia, had spent the latter part of his life in Damascus six centuries earlier. The house that ᶜAbd al-Kader then moved into, which was placed at his disposal by the Governor Izzet Pasha, was the very house where Ibn ᶜArabī died in 638/1240.

Twenty seven years later, at the age of seventy six, ᶜAbd al-Kader, in his turn, died on the night of 18–19 rajab, 1300 (25–26 May 1883).[11] His body was carried to the mosque of the Umayyades, where the prayer for the dead was conducted by the shaikh Mohammed Al-Khānī. He was then taken to the tomb of ᶜIbn Arabī and buried next to him.[12]

Thus, the final phase of the life of the amir, beginning and ending as it did at the tomb of Ibn ᶜArabī, took place under the benediction of the *Doctor Maximus* of Islamic gnosis. This connection did not come about suddenly. Between him, who for his disciples was the "Seal of Mohammedan Sainthood," and ᶜAbd al-Kader there was a profound and ancient bond.

ᶜAbd al-Kader had already cited Ibn ᶜArabī in a work which he wrote around 1850—while he was imprisoned at Amboise—to defend Islam and the Muslims against the attacks of a Catholic priest.[13] One particular fact ought to be emphasized: Ibn ᶜArabī was accused of the darkest heresies by the spokesmen of a militant exotericism and is only read in very limited circles. Not only was he a suspect author, he was also prolific, having composed several hundred treatises, and his major work, the *Futūḥāt al-Makkiyya* amounts to about fifteen thousand pages. In addition, he is a difficult author. Volumes of commentaries have been written on some lines and verses of his. Now, in 1850 at Amboise, ᶜAbd al-Kader was deprived of his library. The precious manuscripts which he had collected had been dispersed or destroyed by an imbecile band of soldiers when the *Smala*, his itinerant capital, was captured. The few Arabic books which he had with him in prison were rather elementary except for the *Ṣaḥīḥ* of Bukhārī, a collection of prophetic traditions.[14] His study of Ibn ᶜArabī, therefore, must date from his youth. For a man who had led a life of combat and wandering since the age of twenty four, the amir demonstrates in this work a culture which was not ordinary. In addition to Ibn ᶜArabī he also cites Avicenna, ᶜIbn Ṭufayl, ᶜIbn Khaldūn, and many others.

But the relation which united ᶜAbd al-Kader and the Shaikh al-Akbar was not simply through books and, in order to understand its nature and measure its importance, we must go even further back. The islamic masters (*mashaikh*, sing. *shaikh*) are necessarily connected to an initiatic lineage through which is transmitted the *baraka*, the spiritual influence. This transmission, which bears some analogy to the apostolic succession as it is known among Roman and Orthodox Christians, is effectuated in diverse ways, one of its modalities being the investiture of the *khirqa*, the "mantle" or the "frock". Although at the beginning all of the initiatic lines were united in the person of the Prophet, who is their common origin, in the course of time they diversified into innumerable branches, each of which bears the imprint of an eminent master who became its eponym. Thus with Ibn ᶜArabī there appears an akbarian *khirqa* ("akbarian" being formed from his title, *al-shaikh al-akbar*), which from then on would be transmitted without interruption from master to disciple. It is distinguished from other lines in that it does not constitute an "order" (*ṭarīqa*, plural *ṭuruq*).[15] Although it is not clandestine, as has been wrongly maintained, it is at least very discreet. Now, documents that have never been published allow us to establish that ᶜAbd al-Kader received the investiture of the akbarian *khirqa,* and that this was indeed a family tradition. It was in fact through his father, Sīdī Muḥyī l-Dīn, that the amir was attached to the akbarian "chain" (*silsila*). Muḥyī l-Dīn in his turn received his own initiation from the amir's grandfather, Sīdī Muṣṭafā, who had been invested with the akbarian *khirqa* in Egypt by a famous personage, the Sayyid Murtaḍa al-Zabīdī (d. 1205/1791).[16]

Since the familial genealogy and the initiatic genealogy coincide, the flowering in Damascus in the person of the amir of an inspired commentator on the *Futūḥāt* no longer appears to be a case of spontaneous generation.[16bis] One could, in passing, meditate on the strange detours whereby—starting from Murcia where Ibn ʿArabī was born, and passing through Damascus where he died, and then to India where the Sayyid Murtaḍā was born—his spiritual heritage made its way to western Islam in Algeria, to return finally to Damascus from which a movement of akbarian renewal began to radiate, the effects of which are still felt today.

We have no indication which would allow us to give a precise date for the attachment of ʿAbd al-Kader to the akbarian *silsila.* Since Sīdī Muḥyī l-Dīn died in 1833, we have, in any case, a *terminus ad quem*: the amir was at most twenty-six years old when he received this investiture. We even hazard the hypothesis that the event took place a little earlier, in the course of one of the most decisive stages in the life of ʿAbd al-Kader, which was his first voyage to the East, around his twentieth year, when he accompanied his father on the pilgrimage, and particularly when he went to Damascus with him, where he became a disciple of a very great master, the Shaikh Khālid al-Naqshbandī.[17]

In any case, the akbarian seed was planted very early and it fell on privileged soil. As a descendant of the prophet, issuing from a line of Sufis—his father had composed a treatise for the guidance of novices, the *Kitāb irshād al murīdin*—and manifesting from his youth the taste for prayer, ʿAbd al-Kader seemed consecrated to the destiny of spiritual master, which he became at Damascus after the divine decree had relieved him from other duties. The normal course from this point of departure to this point of arrival, though uncommon, is foreseeable. This course is the *sulūk*, the way which leads the disciple, step by step, under the direction of a shaikh, until the day when he becomes a master in his turn and guides the following generation.

But the itinerary of ᶜAbd al-Kader was not this ordered course. Numerous passages of the *Kitāb al-Mawāqif*—extracts of which we are presenting here in translation—provide us with elements by which we can reconstitute the overall lines of the spiritual autobiography of the amir. It becomes clear from this that ᶜAbd al-Kader is a *majdhūb*, an "ecstatic" whom God "draws", "attracts" to Him (this is the meaning of the root *J Dh B*) and who thus in one bound leaps over the stages which the *sālik* (the "voyager") crosses one by one in the course of a long, methodical progression.[18] The *majdhūb* is a relatively exceptional case, but it is one which has had, for a long time, its place in the initiatic typology of Islam and which further subdivides itself in a series of derived forms. In the extreme case the *majdhūb* is a "fool of God" (*majnūn, bahlūl*) whose acts totally escape from the control of reason and who, because of this, is no longer subject to legal obligations. He can even be liberated by the divine seizure (*jadhba*) from the ordinary constraints of the human condition, like that Abū ᶜIqāl al-Maghribī that Ibn ᶜArabī speaks of, who, during four years at Mecca, lived in chains without eating or drinking.[19] We see that these characteristics are difficult to reconcile with what we know of the behavior of ᶜAbd al-Kader and the functions which he assumed in the different phases of his existence. But, as Ibn ᶜArabī shows in the same chapter of the *Futūḥāt*, in certain beings the *jadhba* can produce no apparent effect or can manifest itself by barely perceptible exterior signs.

One will find, in several of the texts translated here, the glowing testimony of these moments of ecstatic rapture which were rarely seen by the entourage of the amir (the scene recounted by the profane observer, Léon Roche, is in this respect a priceless document). One will also see—on this point we refer particularly to text 36—the singular modalities which clothe the divine pedagogy: it is by the "projection" (*ilqā*) of the Koranic verses upon his being, whereby each word is rediscovered in its eternal newness, that God directly instructs this pupil without a master.

The absence of a master—a human master—calls for two comments. First, we should remark that according to formal criteria, ᶜAbd al-Kader was from his youth the disciple of several *mashāikh*. The first was his own father, who directed one of the branches of the *ṭarīqa qādiriyya*, the brotherhood whose founder and eponym was the great saint of Baghdad, ᶜAbd al-Qādir al-Jilānī (d. 561/1166). As we have seen, around his twentieth year, he was also connected with the *ṭarīqa naqshbandiyya* at Damascus through shaikh Khālid. From these two masters and probably others as well he must certainly have received not only the *baraka* but also support and directives. Nevertheless, he himself states that his was not the "way of the novitiate" (*ṭarīq al-sulūk*), at least in the beginning.

For, if "the way of ecstatic rapture is the shortest and surest," the way of methodical progression is, according to ᶜAbd al-Kader himself, "the highest and most perfect."[20] In order to attain perfection and become able to guide others, the *majdhūb* must make himself an apprentice and, becoming a *sālik* in his turn, oblige himself to traverse step by step the path whose end he already knows.

This late and paradoxical novitiate, directed and accompanied by the invisible presence of the Shaikh al-Akbar,[21] was to be completed by ᶜAbd al-Kader under the direction of the last of his human masters, Moḥammed al-Fāsī al-Shādhilī.[21bis] Their meeting took place in Mecca where the shaikh Moḥammed al-Fāsī lived and, nine years later, died. Wishing to accomplish the pilgrimage one more time, the amir departed for the Hijaz in the beginning of the month of rajab, 1279 A.H. (January 1863 A.D.).[22]

He first traveled by sea to Alexandria, then he went to Cairo, then Jedda and finally Mecca, where, under the direction of his shaikh, he practiced "the ascetic discipline, the retreat and the spiritual combat." The too short account given by his son indicates that he very quickly traversed the *maqāmāt* ("stations") of the way. But it was at the summit of the *Jabal al-Nūr* (Mount of the Light) in the cave Ḥirāʾ,—

the very one where the prophet received his first revelation—that he arrived at the end of this ascent. Having secluded himself "for many days," he attained, according to his son, "the supreme degree" (*al-rutbat al-kubrā*) and "illumination" (*al-fatḥ al-nūrānī*) "and the fountains of wisdom spring from his tongue."

ᶜAbd al-Kader was to remain in Arabīa for a year and a half. After having accomplished the pilgrimage to Mecca, he went at first to Taïf and then returned to Mecca. After his departure for Taïf, he stopped sending news to his family, who became alarmed and had to address themselves to the amir of Mecca, Abdallāh Pāshā, to reassure themselves of his fate.

At the beginning of the month of rajab 1280—that is, one year after his arrival in the Hijaz—ᶜAbd al-Kader left for Medina. He obtained permission to make a retreat in the house of the first Caliph, Abū Bakr, a house which adjoined the wall of the mosque of the Prophet; and by virtue of a special privilege accorded by him, possessed a window opening onto the interior of the mosque. After this retreat, which lasted two months, the amir remained at Medina, devoting himself to the customary pious visits to the tombs of the Companions, to Mount Ohod and to the mosque of Qubā (an allusion to this stay can be found in text 37). Finally, on the twenty-seventh of the month of Dhūl-Qaᶜada 1280, he joined the caravan of some Syrian pilgrims who had just arrived and accomplished a last pilgrimage to Mecca before returning to Syria.

The *Kitāb al Mawāqif*, the "*Book of Stops*", is the surest evidence of the spiritual science of ᶜAbd al-Kader. The material for this book began to be accumulated from the time when the amir established himself in Damascus in 1856. Although he had not yet encountered at this date the one to whom he would owe the attainment of plenitude, he had already for a long time been a gnostic, an *ᶜārif bi-Llāh*. A succession of visitors came to him. It appears that ᶜAbd al-Kader refused to speak with them about his combats and the episodes which marked his public life. Less than two weeks after his arrival, a trivial incident took place: One of the visitors was accompanied by his son. The son asked his father for permission to leave, which his father granted. The amir, starting from this fact, improvised a Koranic commentary.[23] When he had finished speaking, three of his listeners—the shaikh Moḥammed al-Khānī (whose father had known the amir in the entourage of shaikh Khālid), the shaikh ᶜAbd al-Razzāq al-Bayṭār, and the shaikh Moḥammed al-Ṭanṭāwī—implored him for permission to write down his words. The transcription of these improvised talks was to become the initial kernel of the *Kitāb al-Mawāqif.* These were supplemented by texts written by the amir himself, most often in response to questions which were posed to him on the subject of Koranic verses, words of the prophet or passages from the writings of Ibn ᶜArabī.[24] The collection of these materials had already taken the form of a book during the lifetime of the amir—various manuscripts were in circulation, some of them annotated by him—but the work, as it appears in the two printed editions, certainly does not represent a definitive version.[25] The very title selected by ᶜAbd al-Kader[26] immediately evokes, for historians of Sufism, a celebrated work: the *Mawāqif* of Moḥammed al-Niffarī, who died around 350 A.H.[27] But if Niffarī was the one who introduced the technical term *mawqif* (sing. of *mawāqif*) into the *taṣawwuf,* it was Ibn ᶜArabī who first, in the *Futūḥāt,* where he cites Niffarī on several occasions, explicitly defined the corresponding idea.[28]

For Ibn ᶜArabī there is, between each *Maqām* or each *Manzil*—each "station" or each spiritual "resting place"—and the following *Maqām* or the following *Manzil,* a *mawqif,* a "stop." The *sālik,* the voyager who makes a stop at this intermediate point, receives there from Allah instructions in the rules of spiritual conduct (*adāb*) appropriate to the *Maqām* which he is going to attain and is thus prepared to enjoy the plenitude of the sciences particular to that station. On the other hand, the being who passes directly from one station to another without making the intermediate stop will obtain in the *Maqām* he has arrived at only a global but not a distinctive knowledge of the sciences which are proper to this new "station." According to Ibn ᶜArabī, the progression of the *Ṣāḥib al-mawāqif* is the most difficult and the most challenging, but it is the most fruitful. By the very title of his book, ᶜAbd al-Kader suggests that this is the way which God assigned to him.

If the name, *Kitāb al-Mawāqif*, undoubtedly contains an allusion to the teaching of Ibn ᶜArabī, the content of the book quite explicitly places itself under the authority of the Shaikh al-Akbar. "He is our treasure, from which we draw what we write, whether it be from his spiritual form (*min ruḥāniyyatihi*) or from what he has himself written in his works."[29] In numerous passages,[30] he expresses his certainty that Ibn ᶜArabī is indeed the "Seal of Mohammedan Sainthood"—a function which he defines very precisely in chapter 353 of the *Mawāqif*[31]—and his conviction that in this area the author of the *Fuṣūṣ* is, after the prophets, the one whose counsels are the most profitable for men.

The privileged relation of ᶜAbd al-Kader with Ibn ᶜArabī, symbolized and ritually established by the investiture of the akbarian *khirqa* in the amir's youth, is confirmed by frequent visions reported in the *Mawāqif*. In one of them,[32] Ibn ᶜArabī appears to him at first as a lion and orders him to place his hand in his mouth. When he has vanquished his terror and made this gesture, Ibn ᶜArabī resumes his human form. In another vision, the Shaikh al-Akbar shows his satisfaction with the response which ᶜAbd al-Kader made to certain criticisms directed toward the author of the *Futūḥāt*.[33] In still another, Ibn ᶜArabī expresses his displeasure at seeing ᶜAbd al-Kader addressing some Christians using the ritual formula *al-salām ᶜalaykum*,[34] even though the amir had found a legal justification for this normally forbidden practice. At other times, Ibn ᶜArabī explains certain passages of his works, or studies them with him,[35] or informs him that none of the commentators of the *Fuṣūṣ al-Ḥikam* have perceived its true meaning,[36] or presents him with one of his works,[37] or delivers a sealed writing to him in which, after having broken the seal, he discovers his own image.[38]

This presence of the Shaikh al-Akbar also becomes clear because of the important place which commentaries on certain passages of his treatises have in the *Mawāqif* and the innumerable explicit references to his work. However, a listing of all the references to Ibn ᶜArabī or his works in the

Mawāqif would still be only an incomplete measure of the influence of the Shaikh al-Akbar on ᶜAbd al-Kader. A more thorough search quickly shows that, even where Ibn ᶜArabī is not named, the allusion to his doctrinal teaching and the employment of his technical vocabulary are fundamental characteristics of the *Mawāqif.*[39] Even if we limit ourselves to the most obvious references to Ibn ᶜArabī, it is easy to show that the chapters or passages of the *Mawāqif* devoted to the commentary on various akbarian writings fill a considerable number of pages. These commentaries are always responses to questions posed by those near to the amir. Several lines of the prologue of the *Futūḥāt* are analyzed in a chapter so large that it ended up being considered an independent work, as we have already pointed out in a note.[40] The first sentences of chapter 1 of the *Fuṣūṣ al-Ḥikam* are given sixteen pages of commentary in the *Mawāqif.*[41] By way of comparison, let us note that these sentences (which represent less than one page in the Afīfī edition) are only given two pages of commentary in Qāshānī. Chapter 12 of the *Fuṣūṣ* (seven and a half pages in the Afīfī edition; twelve pages of commentary in Qāshānī, sixteen in Qayṣarī, nineteen in Bālī Effendī) is commented upon by ᶜAbd al-Kader in nearly eighty pages.[42] Chapter 8 of the *Fuṣūṣ,* the one devoted to the prophet Ismāᶜīl (four pages in the Afīfī edition; eight pages of commentary in Qāshānī; sixteen in Qayṣarī; ten in Bālī Effendī) is given thirty-four pages of commentary in the *Mawāqif.*[43] It is noteworthy that ᶜAbd al-Kader begins this in depth interpretation of the *Faṣṣ Ismāᶜīl* by an allusion to a long encounter in the subtle mode with the Shaikh al-Akbar, and by an affirmation of the same kind as that which we have pointed out above. First he explains that one of his "brothers"—he most certainly means a spiritual brotherhood—after having consulted a number of commentaries on the *Faṣṣ Ismāᶜīl* without finding the desired clarifications, had then come to ask him about it. "I responded to him, asking the aid of Allah and basing myself on what had been conferred on me by my lord and master Muḥyī l-dīn [Ibn ᶜArabī] during his life (that is, by his writing) and *after his death* (an allusion to the inspirations received directly from his "spiritual form," his *ruḥāniyya*)."

In the same way we see ᶜAbd al-Kader, in the *Mawāqif,* interpret passages from the *Faṣṣ Luqmān* of the *Fuṣūṣ al-Ḥikam*[44] and a number of difficult texts from the *Futūḥāt.* For instance, from the latter there are commentaries on selected passages from chapters 6,[45] 69,[46] 76,[47] and 373.[48] In addition, ᶜAbd al-Kader returned several times to chapter 73 of the *Futūḥāt,*[49] one of the longest—almost one hundred and forty pages—and also one of the most important, since there is contained in it not only a systematic exposition of the initiatic categories but also the responses which Ibn ᶜArabī, taking up a challenge six centuries old, gives to the famous questionnaire of Ḥakīm Tirmidhī. Tirmidhī was the first in Islam to formulate the notion of the "Seal of Sainthood" and the hundred and fifty-five questions which he poses in his *Kitāb Khatm al-awliyā*[50] constitutes a kind of test permitting the verification of the qualifications of those who would claim the title of "Seal". Therefore, the dialogue which the Shaikh al-Akbar established with him is of interest to anyone who assigns to Ibn ᶜArabī, as ᶜAbd al-Kader does, a major role in the economy of Islamic esotericism.

The multiplicity and breadth of explicit references to the work of Ibn ᶜArabī in the *Mawāqif* are evident to anyone who goes through the three volumes. No less evident, and even more significant, is the author's doctrinal conformity with the teaching of the Shaikh al-Akbar. Conformity, but not conformism: no *taqlīd* ("servile imitation") here. ᶜAbd al-Kader speaks from the fullness of his heart and one who is familiar with the commentators on Ibn ᶜArabī is struck by the difference between his tone and that of the circumspect and laborious glosses of some of the others, especially the later ones—notably Shaᶜrānī. The style of the amir is direct and the most controversial theses of Ibn ᶜArabī are presented and defended without evasions, with the authority of one who draws the truths from their very source. ᶜAbd al-Kader does not evade the problems which certain apparently scandalous pronouncements pose by invoking, as some more prudent commentators did, the probability of malicious interpolations in the copies of the works of Ibn ᶜArabī.[51] It should be noted in addition that ᶜAbd al-Kader is not only an inspired interpreter but is also a scrupulous scholar, and that he took the trouble to send two of his companions to Qonya in order to verify his copy of the *Futūḥāt* by the autograph manuscript of the second redaction (undertaken by Ibn ᶜArabī several years before his death).[52] This is the same manuscript upon which the critical edition currently being prepared in Cairo by Dr. Osman Yahya is based.

Although he is attentive to everything which could put into question the intellectual coherence of the teaching of the Shaikh al-Akbar—which explains his respectful but severe refutation of ᶜAbd al-Karīm al-Jīlī, who is in contradiction with Ibn ᶜArabī on three important questions;[53] and although he limits himself sometimes to citing or paraphrasing some formulation of the author of the *Futūḥāt,* ᶜAbd al-Kader is not a slavish follower devoted to the mechanical repetition of what he has received from his master. On occasion we see him propose an original interpretation of a Koranic verse which can diverge considerably from—without contradicting, however—that held by Ibn ᶜArabī. This is the case for verse ninety-eight of Surah 16 ("When you recite the Koran, take refuge in Allah against Satan the outcast.") which leads him to define briefly, but in a very illuminating way, the distinction between the "Unicity of the direct vision" (*waḥdat al-shuhūd*) and the "Unicity of Being" (*waḥdat al-wujūd*) while at the same time showing their complementarity.[54]

The term *waḥdat al-wujūd*—the "Unicity of Being"—is the one most often used by both advocates and adversaries of Ibn ᶜArabī to designate the cornerstone of his doctrine. We will not go into the problems which this usage presents, but will limit ourselves to noting that this is not the doing of Ibn ᶜArabī himself and to emphasizing that the expression *waḥdat al-wujūd* has a reductionist character which runs the risk of falsifying the understanding of akbarian metaphysics.[55] Therefore we will retain this term simply as a convenient designation validated by long usage. With this reservation, it is evident that acceptance of the *waḥdat al-wujūd* is a condition *sine qua non* of adherence to the akbarian school. We will see in the translations which will follow (in particular in texts 17 through 24) that ᶜAbd al-Kader fully satisfies this condition. "The essence of creatures," he writes in chapter 64,[56] "is not other than the very Essence of Allāh . . . There is only one Essence and only one Reality (*haqīqa*)." This reality, as he points out later on, appears as *Ilāh* (God) in a certain respect and as *ᶜabd* (servant) and *khalq* (creature) in another respect. Just as explicit is chapter 137, which is a commentary on verse 4 of Surah 57: "He is with you wherever you are." He does not interpret this as the theologians usually do as meaning that Allāh is "with you" through His knowledge, but as meaning that there is no being other than the Being of Allāh.[57] The unswerving boldness of these affirmations and other similar ones lead ᶜAbd al-Kader more than once to warn the reader against a false interpretation of his words which might tempt the reader to accuse him of heresy. Unfortunately, to judge by the irrationality and the violence of the attacks on Ibn ᶜArabī and his school throughout the centuries and still in our time, it would seem that this warning has not been fully heeded.[58]

Among the *quaestiones disputatae* which recur most often in the *responsa* of the jurists and in the treatises written for or against Ibn ᶜArabī, we will discuss three by way of example. They have caused a lot of ink to flow. In each case they will confirm the very significant agreement of ᶜAbd al-Kader with the akbarian doctrine. One of these is the final destiny of Firᶜawn, the Pharoah of the story of Moses. In spite of an ambiguous reference at the beginning of chapter 62 of the *Futūḥāt*,[59] the position of the Shaikh al Akbar, as it appears from other texts of the *Futūḥāt* and the *Fuṣūṣ*,[60] is that the *shahāda*, the "testimony of faith" spoken *in extremis* by Firᶜawn is acceptable to God and that Firᶜawn is, therefore, saved. This position, which often embarrasses even the most favorable commentators of Ibn ᶜArabī, is taken up and affirmed by ᶜAbd al-Kader.[61] But what is interesting and shows that this is not a case of blind *taqlīd* with respect to his revered master, is that he says that he bases his support on a direct divine inspiration; and the fact that he gives for the Koranic verses relating to Firᶜawn an interpretation distinct from that of Ibn ᶜArabī.

The second of these *quaestiones disputatae* is that of the eternity of punishment. Although we cannot analyze here the numerous akbarian pronouncements on this problem,[62] let us simply point out that Ibn ᶜArabī emphasizes that, although there are scriptural proofs for the eternal felicity of the elect, there is no *naṣṣ* (decisive text) concerning the eternity of punishment, but only concerning the eternity of the *stay* in the infernal abode, which is not the same thing. He affirms, therefore, that the sufferings of the People of the Fire will have an end: they will remain in the Fire but the *ᶜadhāb*—punishment—will become for them a cause of *istiᶜdhab,* of joy. Thus the last word reverts to the "Divine Mercy which embraces all things." ᶜAbd al-Kader presents at great length the position of Ibn ᶜArabī[63] with all its nuances (which we have had to sacrifice here), and it is manifest that, intuitively, he has taken it as his own. But, if there is no decisive text in the Revelation proving the eternity of punishment, there is also none to support the thesis of the cessation of punishment and, *a fortiori,* of a form of "infernal felicity," so that this can only be considered as a possibility. Several allusions allow us to infer that ᶜAbd al-Kader finally received from God the confirmation of the soundness of the akbarian doctrine about this but that the absence of external proof constrained him not to speak publicly in a categorical manner on such a serious subject. We know from what we have already learned about ᶜAbd al-Kader that this is not from lack of courage but from discretion.

The third of the controversial themes which we will consider for this brief comparison of the teaching of ᶜAbd al-Kader and that of his master offers still another occasion to confirm that the author of the *Mawāqif* is not afraid to expound views unacceptable to Islamic exotericism. This theme is that which we might call the akbarian "universality." This universality is most fully expressed in the celebrated verses of the *Tarjumān al ashwāq* ("The Interpreter of Desires") of Ibn ᶜArabī:[64]

"My heart has become capable of wearing all forms
It is a pasture for gazelles and a convent for monks
A temple for idols and the Kaᶜaba for the pilgrim
It is the tables of the Torah and it is the book of the Koran
I profess the religion of Love, whatever the destination of
its caravans may be
And Love is my law and my faith"

It is also expressed in a poem of the *Futūḥāt* which begins with this verse:

"Created beings have formed various beliefs about God
And for me, I believe everything that they have
believed."[65]

When Ibn ᶜArabī sets forth this aspect of his doctrine, he generally bases it on verse 23 of Surah 17—"And your Lord has decreed that you will worship no one but Him"—which he interprets as meaning that every worshipper, whatever the apparent object of his worship, in fact only worships Allāh.[66] ᶜAbd al-Kader develops the same idea in numerous passages of the *Mawāqif.*[67] For him, as for Ibn ᶜArabī, the foundation *in divinis* of the plurality of beliefs and objects of worship is nothing other than the infinite multiplicity of the divine Names and the inexhaustible diversity of their theophanies. "None of His creatures worships Him in all His aspects; no one is unfaithful to Him in all His aspects," he writes. "No one knows Him in all of His aspects; no one is ignorant of Him in all His aspects. Therefore, each person necessarily knows Him in a certain respect and worships Him in the same respect. Consequently, error does not exist in this world except in a relative manner." "He is the essence of all that is worshipped and in a certain respect, every worshipper worships none other than Him."[68] The man who took the Christians of Damascus under his protection at the time of the Druze revolt in 1860 demonstrated in this way, not only his generosity and courage, but the complete accord between what he does and what he knows.

In a work which appeared in Damascus nearly a century ago,[69] ᶜAbd al-Kader is designated as *wārith al-ᶜulūm al-akbariyya,* the inheritor of the akbarian sciences. He was that in fact and, as the legitimate heir, he transmitted this heritage in his turn. We have already made reference to a movement of akbarian renewal. We cannot describe this in detail here or show all of its consequences. But certain of its effects can be seen: we owe to it the first edition of the *Futūḥāt* of Ibn ᶜArabī, financed by the amir himself in 1274 A.H. Following this first impulse, other works of Ibn ᶜArabī appeared in the course of the last hundred years, in editions which, although often imperfect, are still precious. Other manifestations are discernible which are more discreet but are even more significant: in particular, that sudden flowering toward the end of the last century of the *nisba akbariyya* among certain Egyptian and Syrian spiritual masters who add to their name the qualification *al-akbarī* "the akbarian."[70] One might conclude from this phenomenon that there was a resurgence of a *ṭarīqa akbariyya* after a long period of semi-clandestine existence. This term implies the existence of a structured organization—of an "order" or a "brotherhood," according to the usual translations of the word *ṭarīqa*. However, though it is possible to point out an occasional appearance of *ṭuruq(s)* bearing the name *akbariyya,* it is difficult to discover any precise historical link between them, and their characteristics are apparently very different. In a case of this type, this denomination has a fairly provisional character and, in a certain way, it complements that which defines the identity of the organization in question. It appears most frequently in certain branches of two *ṭuruq(s),* the *shādhiliyya* and the *naqshbandiyya*. It is noteworthy that ᶜAbd al-Kader was attached to both of them and that the influence of Ibn ᶜArabī is most perceptible precisely in the branches of these two *ṭuruq(s),* or offshoots of them. It is even more remarkable that the study of available historical facts, especially the *silsila*-s, shows that all the *mashāikh* who, openly or not, have played a role in this akbarian restoration have been, directly or indirectly, connected with ᶜAbd al-Kader.[71]

It seems then that these two *ṭuruq(s)* were, in a privileged, but certainly not exclusive, way chosen as supports for the spiritual influence of the Shaikh al-Akbar. But the *baraka* of Ibn ᶜArabī, regularly transmitted from generation to generation, has been able to act on very diverse organizations although they don't express this relation with the Shaikh al-Akbar by any special name, and even though the majority of their members may not be conscious of this relationship. Indeed, this discreet diffusion through and across the pre-existing initiatic structures, each of which maintains its own identity and characteristics, is the result of the very nature of the function of Ibn ᶜArabī. As the "Seal of Mohammedan Sainthood," he sums up and preserves the totality of the forms of wisdom and sainthood which had been deposited in Islam and, in contrast to other masters who represent only particular aspects of this totality, his special intervention cannot be enclosed within the limits of a "brotherhood".[72]

In the tumult of the *nahda*—the "Arab renaissance"—this other renaissance, contemporary with it, is in danger of passing unnoticed.[73] It arises from an Islam of silence, because it is an Islam of the inexpressible. Its influence is felt in very limited circles (but number is of no importance here); and, in particular, it is felt in circles increasingly distinct from the intelligentsia observable to the chronicler or, later on, to the historian.

For the historian, men like shaikh Aḥmad b. Sulaymān al-Khalīdī al-Tarabulsī, shaikh Aḥmad Gümüshkhānevī,[74] and shaikh Moḥammed al-Ṭanṭāwī—who during this time were important links in the transmission of the spiritual heritage of Ibn ᶜArabī—are remembered, if at all, in a footnote. Others do not even receive this dubious honor and their names are preserved only in the collective memory of the *ṭuruq*. When one or another of these masters escapes from this quasi-anonymity—the case of ᶜAbd al-Kader is clearly the most remarkable in this respect—it is for reasons which do not arise from his special function. If, for example, another major protagonist of this akbarian current, the shaikh ᶜAbd al-Raḥmān ᶜIllaysh, is better known and more studied than some of the others, it is due to his role as a Malikite mufti and to his political tribulations.

The effects of the movement of which we are speaking, and of which ᶜAbd al-Kader is the pivot, are necessarily discreet. The very nature of the teaching of Ibn ᶜArabī does not permit it to be otherwise. One should not believe, however, that these effects were only felt in the Middle East. That would already be a great deal. But, the extreme porousness of the Islamic community should not be underestimated and we have been able to discover traces of it in the most distant locations, even as far as present day China.

One question arises, however. In this age, in which the decadence of traditional Islam seems to be at its peak, we may be surprised at the renewed flowering of the the heritage of the Master *par excellence* of the spiritual sciences. ᶜAbd al-Kader gives a response to this question and he finds this response, quite naturally, in the work of the Shaikh al-Akbar himself.[75] "The entire universe," writes Ibn ᶜArabī, "fell asleep at the time of the death of the Messenger of Allah." And, according to a famous *ḥadīth* in which Allāh descends to the heaven of this lower world in the last third of each night, Ibn ᶜArabī adds: "We are presently in the last third of this night of the sleep of the universe. Now, the theophany which gives the graces, the sciences, and the perfect knowledge in their most complete forms is that of the last third of the night, for it is the closest since it appears in the heaven of this lower world. That is why the science of this community is more perfect at the approach of its end than it ever was in its middle or after it began with the death of the Messenger of Allāh—on him be Grace and Peace!"

The indications which we have given concerning the genesis of the *Kitāb al-Mawāqif* makes it clear that it is not a treatise where the order of chapters would reflect the progressive exposition of an organized doctrine. Although there are sometimes rather imprecise references to previous pages, each *mawqif* or 'stop'—there are 372 in all, varying greatly in length—constitutes an autonomous whole. The *mawāqif* are not given titles, but generally open with a Koranic citation or a *hadīth* of the Prophet.

The thirty-nine texts which we have translated here were chosen either because they present the major themes of the teaching of ᶜAbd al-Kader or establish the points of reference of his spiritual autobiography. We have given them titles to facilitate their identification and have arranged them in six groups according to their main theme. We are aware that this classification is somewhat arbitrary and that the interdependence of the ideas expressed in this brief anthology could justify other arrangements. One might even maintain that the 372 *mawāqif* have one single theme, which is the universal presence of God.

We have noted and deplored the absence of a critical edition (see note 25). Our translation is based on the second edition (three volumes totaling 1416 pages). Common sense and a long familiarity with the writings of ᶜAbd al-Kader have led us to make some corrections—indicated in footnotes—in a text often disfigured by the errors of copyists or misreadings by the editor (the amir was, after all, fairly negligent in the way he wrote, as is shown by the spelling errors which are found in some of his letters). Whether these corrections are well founded or not can only be verified by a methodical comparison with the best manuscripts.

As a conclusion, we have given the translation of a short poem taken, not from the *Kitāb al-Mawāqif* but from the *Dīwān* edited (not very critically) in Damascus around 1966 by Dr. Mamdūḥ Ḥaqqī.

In the notes to this translation, we were only able to make succint comments and explanations concerning the many implicit and explicit references to the teaching of Ibn ᶜArabī in the *Kitāb al-Mawāqif*. Readers who wish to go more deeply into this subject can refer to *The Sufi Path of Knowledge* by William C. Chittick (SUNY, 1989) and two of my books, *Seal of the Saints* (Islamic Texts Society, Cambridge, UK, 1993) and *An Ocean without Shore* (SUNY, 1993). The biography of Ibn ᶜArabī by Claude Addas, *Quest for the Red Sulphur, the Life of Ibn ᶜArabī* (Islamic Texts Society, Cambridge, UK, 1993) is also available in English.

I am especially grateful to my daughter Claude—author of the book mentioned above—for the help she has given me. Our readings together and the exchanges which followed them have been invaluable to me. My daughter Agnes, for her part, took on the formidable task of transcribing a manuscript which was often barely legible. But my gratitude goes to all my family—my wife and my children were associated with the gestation of this work from the very beginning. It was done for them and for the children of our children. Thus it would be to them that this work would have been dedicated if I had not first to honor a debt which is also theirs.

THE BOOK OF STOPS

I

On the Way

1

God has Stolen my "I" from Me . . .

God has stolen my [illusory] "I" from me and has brought me near to my [real] "I", and the disappearance of the earth has brought the disappearance of heaven.[1] The whole and the part have merged. The vertical (*ṭūl*) and the horizontal (*ᶜarḍ*) are annihilated.[2] The supererogatory work has returned to the obligatory work[3] and the colors have returned to the pure primordial white.[4] The voyage has reached its end and everything other than Him has ceased to exist. All attribution (*iḍāfāt*), every aspect (*iᶜtibārāt*) and all relation (*nisab*) being abolished, the original state is re-established. "Today I lower your lineage and raise up Mine!"[5]

Then the saying of Ḥallāj was spoken to me, with the difference that he pronounced it himself, whereas for me it was spoken without my expressing it myself. This saying is understood and accepted by those who are worthy, and misunderstood and rejected by those overcome by ignorance.[6]

Mawqif 7.

2

The Two Ways

And we have already given you the oft-repeated seven.

(Kor. 15:87)[7]

If one whom Allāh, in His mercy, has gratified by making Himself known to him and by making known to him the essential reality of the higher world and lower world, in spite of that begins to desire the vision of the hidden world (*ʿālam al-ghayb*), of the absolute Imagination (*al-khayāl al-muṭlaq*),[8] and of everything which escapes sensible perception and consists of illusory forms, of pure relations devoid of objective existence and which have no other reality than that of the true Being (*al-wujūd al-ḥaqq*)—for they are none other than His manifestations, His attributes, His relations, which are objectively non-existent—he is in error and goes contrary to the principles of spiritual behavior.

I am one of those whom Allāh, through His mercy, has gratified by making Himself known to them and by making known to them the essential reality of the universe through ecstatic rapture rather than by means of an initiatic voyage (*ʿalā tariqati l-jadhba, lā ʿalā ṭarīq al-sulūk*).[9] For the "voyager" (*al-sālik*) the sensible world is unveiled first, then the world of imagination. Then he rises in spirit as far as the heaven of the lower world, then to the second heaven, then to the third, and so on until he reaches the divine throne. During the whole course of this journey he nonetheless continues to be among those beings who are spiritually veiled until such time as Allāh makes Himself known to him and tears away the final veil. Afterwards, he returns by the same route and sees things differently than he did when he saw them on his first journey. It is only then that he knows them with a true knowledge.

This way, even though it is the highest and most perfect, is indeed long for the voyager and exposes him to grave dangers.[10] All of the successive unveilings are in fact so many trials. Will the voyager allow himself to be stopped by them or not? Some are stopped at the first unveiling, or at the second, and so on until the last of these tests. If he is one of those whom divine providence has predestined for success, if he perseveres in his quest, stays firm in his resolution, avoids everything which does not lead to the goal, he achieves victory and deliverance. If not, he is rejected from the degree at which he has stopped and sent back to the one he departed from, losing at the same time this world and the other. It is for this reason that the author of the "Sentences" said,[11] "The forms of the creatures do not present themselves to the disciple without the heralds of the Truth intervening to say to him, 'What you search for is before you! We are nothing but temptation! Do not make yourself guilty of infidelity!' " One of the masters has also said on this subject:

> Each time that you see the spiritual degrees display their brilliance
> Step aside, just as we have stepped aside!

When such beings arrive finally at the knowledge which was their goal, these unveilings are removed from them at the end of their journey. As for the way of ecstatic rapture, it is the shortest and surest. Is there for the sage anything which equals its certainty?

It is to these two ways that God alludes in the verse: "And you will know then who is on the straight path and who is led." (Kor. 26:135). This means: then it will be revealed to you who are those who have arrived at the knowledge of God by traveling the straight, middle road, without detour, that is to say, the way of Allāh and his Prophet, and who are those who were "led"; that is who arrived at the knowledge of God without accomplishing the initiatic voyage step by step, nor anything of this kind, but by rapture in God and the support of His mercy. One who is in this situation is the "desired" (*al-murād*),[12] a term which is defined as meaning "he whose will (or whose 'desire' [*irāda*]) has been torn away," and everything has been disposed in advance in his favor. He crosses all the forms and all the stages without effort. The verse does not mention those who do not belong to either of these categories and thus do not arrive at the knowledge of Allāh, either by initiatic voyage or by ecstatic rapture.

One day, the thought came to my mind: "If only Allāh had unveiled for me the world of the absolute Imagination!" This state persisted for two days and provoked in me a state of contraction (*qabḍ*).[13] While I was invoking Allāh, He ravished me from myself and projected His word onto me: "A messenger has come to you from yourself" (or: "from your own souls" *min anfusikum,* Kor. 9:139) and I understood that God had pity on what was happening to me. In this state of contraction, in the course of one of the ritual prayers, I addressed the following request to Him: "Oh my God, make me realize what the People of the Proximity have realized and lead me in the way of the People of ecstatic rapture." Then I heard in myself, "I have already done that!" I awoke then from my unconsciousness and I knew concerning what I had requested either that the moment for obtaining it had not yet arrived or that the divine Wisdom had decreed that I would not obtain it and that I was therefore in error in requesting it. I was like one whom the king summons to his court and invites to sit next to him to keep him company and converse with him; who, in spite of that, desires to see the king's porters, his stable boys and his servants, or to amuse himself in the markets. Therefore I turned again to Allāh and asked him to make me realize, regarding knowledge and service of Him, the purpose for which I had been created.

A similar thought came to me another time when I found myself at Medina—may God's blessing be upon it!

I was preparing myself to invoke God when he ravished me from myself and projected his word upon me: "And we have already given you the oft-repeated seven and the glorious Koran. Therefore do not direct your gaze toward that whose enjoyment we have already conceded to certain groups from among them!" (Kor. 15:87–88)[14] When I recovered my senses I said, "That is enough for me! That is enough!" This preoccupation then disappeared completely from my mind and I did not remember it until much later.

Mawqif 18.

3

On Pure Love

God said to one of his servants,[15] "Do you claim to love Me? If so, know that your love for Me is only a consequence of My love for you. You love that which is. But I loved you then when you were not!"

Then He said to him, "Do you claim that you search to come near to Me and to lose yourself in Me? But I search for you much more than you search for Me! I searched for you in order that you should be in My presence without any intermediary, the Day when I said, 'Am I not your Lord?' (Kor. 7:172);[16] then, when you were only spirit (*rūḥ*). Then, when you had a body, you forgot Me and I searched for you again, sending you My messengers. All that was love of you for you and not for Me."

Again He said to him, "What do you think you would do if, when you found yourself in a state of extreme hunger, thirst and exhaustion, I called you to Me, offering you My paradise with its Houris, its palaces, its rivers, its fruits, its pages, its cup-bearers, after having forewarned you that near me you would not find any of that?"

The servant answered, "I would take refuge in You against You."[17]

Mawqif 112.

4

Perfect Adoration

> *But no: it is the jinn that they worshipped, and it is in them that most of them believed.*
>
> (Kor. 34:41)[18]

On a certain night I found myself in the sacred mosque in the vicinity of the *maṭāf*[19] facing the Kaᶜaba and devoting myself to the invocation (*dhikr*). Everyone was sleeping. The voices were silent. Suddenly, people came and sat next to me, on my right and on my left, and began to invoke God. A question came to my mind: "Which among us is best directed toward the way of God?" Soon after this thought had come to me, God ravished me from the world and from myself, then projected his word upon me: "But no, it is the jinn that they worshipped".[20]

I knew then that the worship of these people was tainted by personal desires and anxieties inspired by passions. Then I said to myself, in accord with the teaching of the spiritual masters (*al-muḥaqqiqīn min ahli-Llāh*): whoever adores Allāh through the fears of the fires of hell or in order to gain Paradise, whoever invokes Him in order that his share in the goods of the world be enlarged, or so that people should turn their faces toward him in order that he be glorified, or to avoid the evil which an oppressor afflicts upon him; or further, if he has heard a *ḥadīth* of the Prophet according to which he who accomplishes a certain pious work, or recites a certain invocation, will receive from

God some recompense—whoever does this, his adoration is tainted, and it will not be acceptable to God except by virtue of His grace and of His generosity. Nevertheless, if the things which I have mentioned do not constitute the aim of the pious act, if the man only thinks of them as consequences of what he has accomplished and does not act with the purpose of obtaining them, there is no harm in that.

God said, "Whoever hopes to encounter his Lord, let him do pious works and, in the adoration of his Lord, not associate any being with Him." (Kor. 18:110) The things which I have mentioned are the "beings" which are associated with God. Now, God is, of all those that are associated in adoration, the One who absolutely transcends all association. That is why He prescribed to all His servants that they adore Him with a perfectly pure faith which implies the desire for no other recompense than His face. It is He who gives them the gracious gift of recompense and spiritual degrees, and preserves them from evil or blamable deeds. Everything that one seeks in adoration other than God is an "associated," that is to say an unreal (*maᶜdūm*) and hidden (*mastūr*) thing, a simple name which does not correspond to any "named." God alludes to this when He says, "But no, it is the jinn that they worshipped." In fact, the word *jinn* is etymologically related to the word *ijtinān*, which expresses the idea of being hidden (*istitār*). Everything which is other than Allāh is "hidden" in non-being, even if it appears to spiritually veiled beings to be endowed with existence. But the sage does not concern himself with what is non-being and does not make it the aim of his acts. That is why I say, and it is Allāh—may He be exalted!—who speaks with my tongue: he who does not follow the way of the initiates and does not acquire their spiritual sciences in order to know himself will not attain perfect purity in adoration even if he is the most pious, the most scrupulous, the most ascetic of men; the most energetic in retreat far from creatures and in the pursuit of a hidden life; the most perspicacious in the examination of the ruses of the passionate soul and its secret faults. But if the divine Mercy grants him the knowledge of himself, then his adoration will be pure; and, for him, paradise and hell, recompense, spiritual degrees and all created things will be as though God had never created them. He will not accord them any importance, nor will he take them into consideration, except to the extent that it is prescribed by the divine Law and Wisdom. For then he will know Who is the sole Agent.

In fact, contrary to the opinion of the Muᶜtazilites, the servant does not act or create through his own voluntary acts. Neither does he act under divine constraint as the *Jabriyya* maintain. Nor is there in him some portion of free will by virtue of which he could be considered as an agent, as Māturīdī thinks. Further, there is no "acquisition" (*kasb*) of the act by the creature in the sense that the occurrence of the act would be produced by his will and his free choice, without there being either the creation of the act by the creature or by absolute divine constraint; the truth being found between the two, as in the opinion of the Ashᶜārites. Neither is it the case that there is effectuation of the act by God, the action of the servant only producing an effect through the legal qualification of that act as "good" or "bad," as was maintained by the Imām al-Ḥaramayn.[21] Nor is there anything more to hold to in the opinions of all the other categories of philosophers or theologians.[22]

The attribution of acts to the servant from the point of view of the sacred Law; and the correspondence between reward and punishment on the one hand, and good and bad actions on the other, should be treated in another way, as we have discussed in various passages of this book.

Mawqif 4.

5

Oh, thou, Soul at Peace . . .

Oh, thou, soul at peace, return unto thy Lord, well-pleased and well-pleasing,
Enter among my Servants
And enter into My paradise.

(Kor. 89:27–29)

This soul whom the Lord calls upon in this way, describing it as "at peace, well-pleased and well-pleasing," is ordered by Him—and this order is in fact an authorization, a permission and a mark of honor—to enter among His servants, those whom He expressly takes to Himself, those who have been chosen by Him. These are those souls who know their true relation to servitude and Lordship, that is to say, those who know that in naming the "servant" one is designating nothing other than a particular manifestation of the Lord as it is conditioned by the characteristics of the servant: the essential Reality is "Lord," the exterior is "Servant." The servant is a "Lord" manifested in the form of a "Servant" and, in the appearance of a worshipper, it is Himself who adores Himself.

For the servant, the entry into His paradise (*fī jannatihi*) consists [in conformity with the sense of the root JNN] in becoming hidden (*ijtinān*) in His Essence. He who attains this has traversed the veils of the creatures and of the divine Names. The illusory creatural determinations which have no reality except at the level of sensible perceptions have vanished for him. Without these perceptions there would be only the pure, absolute Being.

Then, the creature being "enveloped" by God, his ipseity disappears—with respect to its existential status, but not with respect to the permanent reality.[23] On the other hand, when the divine Ipseity is "enveloped" by the creature, it remains in its immutable transcendence and is never affected by any change.

This call and this divine order are nevertheless not addressed to the soul until it has passed beyond the stage of the "science of certainty" to attain that of the "reality of certainty,"[24] thanks to the authentic spiritual experience and to perfect unveiling; and that in light of the following two things:

In the first place it is necessary that the soul have the certainty that God is a free Agent who, in conformity with His knowledge and His wisdom, does that which is proper, in the proper way, in the proper measure, at the proper moment; with the consequence that, in whatever respect or from whatever point of view, there could be no act more perfect or wise than that,[25] and that if the servant had access to the divine Wisdom and to the knowledge of what the circumstances demand, he would not chose to perform any act but that. From the moment that the soul possesses this certainty it attains the station of "pleasure" in the will of Allāh, it is "at peace" and the accomplishment of the divine decrees does not shake its immovable serenity.

In the second place, it should have the certainty, based on spiritual experience and intuitive unveiling, that God is the only Agent of everything which proceeds from his creatures without any exception. If the creature plays, with respect to a given act, the role of cause, of condition, or of hindrance, in reality it is God who "descends" from the degree of His absoluteness—without ceasing to be absolute—in this form which one calls condition, cause or hindrance. He does what He does by means of this form. He could dispense with it if He desired to act without it, but such is His free choice and His wisdom. The act is thus attributed at first view to this form, whereas in reality it belongs solely to Him, alone, without associate.

Thus the soul will be "pleased" near its Lord since no act can proceed from it, and as a consequence nothing can cause it to cease being pleased. The pleasure and the love of God for His creatures constitute the original state. His pleasure and love are the means by which He has brought His creatures into existence and are the cause of that bringing into existence. He who knows that he possesses neither being nor act rediscovers himself in that original state of pleasure and divine love.

May Allāh, by His grace and His generosity, place us and our brothers among those who are embraced by the call of this verse! So be it![26]

Mawqif 180.

6

What then has He Lost who has Found You?

> *And if you are patient—certainly that* (huwa) *is better* (khayr) *for those who are capable of being patient.*
>
> (Kor. 16:126)

In this verse, Allāh consoles his patient servants in their trials by announcing that He Himself is the substitute and the replacement of that which they have lost and which was pleasing to their natural dispositions. In effect, being patient consists in constraining the soul to accept that which is repugnant to it. The soul experiences an aversion for everything which is not in accord with its predisposition in the present instant, even if it knows that it will be beneficial for it later on. The psychic (*nafsānī*) and natural suffering which souls feel when they are thus constrained cannot be repelled unless a powerful and dominating spiritual state takes charge of them and makes them forget what causes their sufferings and what would have given them pleasure. It is because man by himself cannot escape from this suffering that the greatest saints have wept, groaned, sighed, asked for help and prayed that they be spared these sufferings. It is not the same for spiritual suffering (*rūḥānī*) which man is capable of repelling. Thus one sees the saints rejoice inwardly, happy, satisfied, certain that Allāh has chosen for them that which is best, tranquil in face of the [spiritual] suffering which touches them. Nothing is displeasing or bad by essence, but only in relation to the "receptacles" and to the predispositions of the physical bodies. If one considers beings in relation to their metaphysical realities (*al-ḥāqāʾiq al-ghaybiyya*), everything which happens to them is appropriate for them. Even further, nothing happens to them which is not demanded by their essential nature.

Allāh has thus announced to those who patiently bear the loss of that which pleases them—health, riches, greatness, security, possessions and children—that "He" [for this is the proper sense of the pronoun *huwa* rendered above as "that" in conformity with the way the verse is usually understood] is better (*khayr*) for them than that which they have lost; for they know that "He" [who is the Name of the supreme absolutely unconditioned Essence] is their inseparable reality and their necessary refuge, and that the pleasing things that they have lost were pure illusions (*umūr wahmiyya khayāliyya*).

Allāh—may he be exalted!—has used here the term *la-huwa* "certainly He." Now, the *huwa* is the unknowable Reality which cannot be grasped, which cannot be named or described. It is the unmanifested Principle of all manifestation, the Reality of all reality. It does not cease nor is it transformed, does not divide or change. *Huwa* is not used here as a third person pronoun (the absent person) which is grammatically related to a first person (one who speaks), and to a second (one to whom one speaks) [for this would imply a multiplicity, which is infinitely transcended by the metaphysical *huwa*]. Allāh did not say *la-anā* "certainly I," for the pronoun *anā* has a determinative character since it implies presence. Now, everything which is determined is, by that very fact, limited.

As for the term "better" (*khayr*) it is [grammatically] a relative term which therefore supposes a comparison between two terms which have something in common between them. Certainly, in this case no comparison is conceivable nor is there anything in common, but God speaks to His servants in the language which they know, and He leads them in ways which are familiar to them. If not, what is there in common between being and non-being? And how can one compare reality with illusion?

He who has found Allāh has lost nothing, and he who has lost Allāh has found nothing. This is what one reads in the prayers of Ibn ᶜAṭā Allāh:[27]

> What then has he found who has lost You?
> And what then has he lost who has found You?

Mawqif 220.

7

On the Necessity of a Spiritual Master

Oh, you who believe! Fear Allāh, and seek a means of access to Him, and struggle on His way; perhaps you will succeed!

(Kor. 5:35)[28]

This verse contains an indication of the course of the Way which leads to knowledge.

In the first place, God commands believers to practice the fear of Him (*al-taqwā*). This corresponds to what is called, among us, the "station of repentance" (*maqām al-tawba*), which is the basis of all progress on the Way and the key which permits one to arrive at the "station of realization" (*maqām al-taḥqīq*). To him who is granted the "station of repentance" is granted arrival at the goal, and to him to whom it is refused arrival at the goal is refused. As was said by one of the masters: "Those who do not arrive at the goal (*al-wuṣūl*), it is because they did not respect the principles (*al-uṣūl*)."

After that God says to us: "And seek a means of access to Him." That is to say: after having mastered the "station of repentance" by conforming with all of its conditions, seek a means of access. The means is a master whose initiatic lineage (*nisba*) is faultless,[29] who has a veritable knowledge of the Way, of the deficiencies which obstruct it and the illnesses which prevent the arrival at Gnosis; and who possesses a proven science of healing, and of the temperaments and dispositions and their appropriate remedies. There is absolute unanimity among the People of Allāh on the fact that, in the Way toward Gnosis, a "means of access" (*wasīla*), that is to say, a master, is indispensable. Books can in no way take the place of a master, at least from the time that supernatural inspirations (*al-wāridāt*), illuminations of theophanies (*bawāriq al-tajalliyyāt*) and spiritual events (*al-wāqiᶜāt*) begin. When that happens, it becomes necessary to explain to the disciple what in all that should be accepted or rejected; what is sound and what is tainted.[30] However, at the beginning of the Way he can be satisfied with books which deal with pious behavior and with spiritual combat in its most general sense.

"And struggle on His Way": this is an order to do battle after having found a master. It is a matter of a special holy war (*jihād*), which is carried out under the command of the master and according to the rules which he prescribes. One cannot have confidence in a spiritual combat carried on in the absence of the master, except in very exceptional cases, for there is not a unique holy war carried on in a unique manner. The dispositions of beings are varied, their temperaments are very different one from another and something which is profitable for one can be harmful for another.

Mawqif 197.

8

The Two Deaths

Allāh—may He be exalted!—said:

Is it not to Allāh that everything will return?

(Kor. 42:53)

It is to Him that everything will come back

(Kor. 11:123)

And you will be led back to Him

(Kor. 10:56)

It is to Him that you will return

(Kor. 6:60)

as well as other similar words.

Know that the becoming of each thing leads it back to God and that it is to Him that it returns. This return of the creatures to Him takes place after the Resurrection and this takes place after the annihilation of creatures. But as the Prophet said—on Him be Grace and Peace!—"For him who dies, the day of Resurrection has already dawned."

There are two kinds of death, the death which is inevitable and common to all beings, and the death which is voluntary and particular to certain ones of them only. It is this second death which is prescribed for us in the words of the Messenger of Allāh: "Die before you die." The resurrection is accomplished for him who dies this voluntary death.[31] His affairs return to God and they are but one. He has returned to God and he sees Him through Him. As the Prophet said—on him be Grace and Peace!—according to a tradition reported by Tabarānī, "You will not see your Lord before being dead" and that is because, in the contemplation of this dead-resurrected one, all creatures are annihilated, and for him only one thing exists, one Reality only. Whatever will be the lot of the believers in their posthumous states is prefigured in one degree or another in this life for the initiates. The "return" of things—considered in relation to [the diversity of] their forms—to Allāh and the end of their becoming, expresses only a change of cognitive status and not at all a modification of the reality. For him who dies and achieves the resurrection, the multiple is one, by reason of its essential unity; and the One is multiple, by reason of the multiplicity in Him of relations and aspects.

The essences (*al-aᶜyān*)—which some also call the substances (*al-jawāhir*)—never disappear. The "new creation,"[32] which is permanent in this world and in the other, only concerns the forms, which are only accidents. And everything which is not the absolute Being—which belongs to God—is accident.

Mawqif 221.

9

When the Sight will be Dazed . . ."

When the sight will be dazed, when the moon will be eclipsed, when the sun and moon will be in conjunction, on that day man will say: 'Where to flee?' But there is no refuge.

(Kor. 75:7–11)

What the commentators have said about these verses is well known and there is nothing to change there.[33] But there is, beyond that, a subtle allusion and another aspect to consider.

"When the sight will be dazed"; when it will be stunned and perplexed. This relates to the moment when the theophanies begin,[34] for the being has no previous knowledge of what he is now contemplating, no familiarity with what he is seeing.

The "moon" symbolizes the servant in his contingency, and the "eclipse" his disappearance: that is to say, the evidence that his being is borrowed and does not belong to him himself for he "is" only in a metaphorical way.

Thus all this indicates obtaining the station of "union" (*maqām al-jam*ᶜ), which consists in seeing God without seeing the creature.[35] This is a dangerous station, where the risk of stumbling is great. It is a critical position for everyone, with the exception of him to whom the station belongs by virtue of an effective spiritual realization (*dhawqan*); for God assists such a one, leads him to a safe place and shelters him from the divine wrath. But the one who only attains this station through books, or who has only received the knowledge from the mouths of imperfect masters, is very close to being lost and has little chance of escaping. Satan has easy access to him and has powerful arguments at his disposal. The devil continually induces him, bit by bit, into error saying, "God is your essential reality. You are not other than Him! Do not exhaust yourself in acts of adoration. They were only instituted for the vulgar who have not attained this station, who do not know what you know, and who have not arrived at the point where you have arrived." Then he permits to him the things which were prohibited saying; "You are one of those to whom it was said: do as you wish, for paradise belongs to you by right."[36] This man then becomes an atheist, libertine, incarnationist. "He leaves religion as the arrow leaves the game which it has passed through, leaving no trace."[37]

The sun symbolizes the Lord—may He be exalted!—just as the moon symbolizes the servant. Their "conjunction" symbolizes the degree of the "union of the union" (*jamʿ al-jamʿ*), which is the ultimate degree, the greatest deliverance and the supreme felicity; and consists in seeing at the same time the creation subsisting by God, and God manifesting Himself by His creation. For God manifests Himself only by the creation, and the creation without God would not manifest itself. Seen from this station, no form can exist without this conjunction, but this means neither incarnation, unification nor mixture,[38] since Allāh is the Reality of everything which is (*fa-inna Llāha ʿaynu kulli mawjūd*) and since there cannot be a creature who would be empty of the Being of God, nor can there be a God who would be empty of the being of His creation.

The gnostic then asks "Where to flee?" because of the violence of the perplexity provoked in him by the multiplicity of the theophanies: their diversity, their fleeting character, the rapidity with which they disappear, the abundance of the divine descents (*tanazzulāt*) which stun the intellect and plunge it in stupor—all that even though these theophanies proceed from a unique source.

"But there is no refuge"—there is no shelter, no way out. The gnostic who would leave this state to find repose is warned that the repose and the Gnosis are only found precisely where he is. The perplexity increases as the divine descents increase, but it is these divine descents which are the source of spiritual knowledge. This is why the foremost of the gnostics, our Prophet—on Him be Grace and Peace!—said "Oh Allāh, augment my perplexity with regard to Thee!"[39]

Mawqif 320.

10

On the Prayer by Day and the Prayer by Night

> *Do not recite your prayer in a loud voice, yet do not recite it in a soft voice, but search for a middle way between the two.*
>
> (Kor. 17:110)

This means: do not recite the totality of the Koranic recitation prescribed in the ritual prayer in a loud voice and do not recite it totally in a soft voice either, but try to find a middle way between an entirely vocal recitation and an entirely silent recitation. This consists of making recitation in your ritual prayers sometimes silently and sometimes in a loud voice, as is explained by the prophetic *sunna*.[40]

I was asked about the esoteric meaning of this among the people of our way. At that time I did not have any knowledge on this subject and I limited myself to responding with that which constitutes half of knowledge, by saying simply, "I do not know."

Later, I was inspired with the secret sense of this rule. It is this: the total reality divides itself between non-manifestation, which is the nature of the divine Essence, and manifestation, which is the prerogative of the divine Names. Thus it is incumbent on the servant to be perpetually between two contemplations, on that which is hidden, having to do with the Essence, and on that which is apparent, having to do with the Names. Accordingly, God gave the servant two eyes, one exterior, one interior. With the interior eye he looks at the non-manifested; with the exterior eye he looks at the manifested. Thus he is like an isthmus (*barzakh*)[41] between these two worlds and should not become entirely swallowed up in one to the exclusion of the other. If he does, he is like a one eyed man. Now, because of the symbolic correspondence between night and the darkness of the Essence—which is the sea of Darkness—he who is completely surrounded by it must certainly perish. Recitation in a loud voice is manifestation (*ẓuhūr*). It has, therefore, been prescribed for those who pray at night in order that the Darkness of the non-manifested should not totally overpower him and that he should maintain a link with the manifested so that he would not be separated from it in every respect. If it were otherwise, the darkness of the non-manifested would swallow him up and one of two things would occur. Either he would disappear in the company of those who are submerged in the darkness of the Essence and for whom it is a case of an effective spiritual realization (*dhawqan*)—for them, all legal obligation is annulled since they have left behind them the light of the divine Names and the faculty of discernment which is the condition for legal responsibility; or he would go to his perdition with all those who have been submerged in the unicity of the Essence only by means of a theoretical knowledge, but who have retained the faculty of discernment. The presence of this faculty makes respect for the legal prescriptions obligatory. These become libertines and perish. "And we take refuge in Allah against scarcity after abundance."[42]

In a vision between waking and sleep, it was said to me; "The disobediences and infractions all come from the Essence." That can be understood in two ways. The way which interests us here is the following: The being who is submerged by the vision of the one Essence—which transcends the Names and their operations—and who is thus deprived of the vision of the degree from which the Messengers bring the definition of the licit and the illicit, from which the sacred Books are revealed, from which the laws are instituted; this being [is apt to accomplish acts which],[43] if they were performed by someone other than him, would be legal faults.

There is, on the other hand, a symbolic correspondence between the day and the degree from which the epiphanies of the divine Names—which are lights, stars, suns and moons[44]—proceed. Recitation in a soft voice being non-manifestation, it is prescribed to him who prays in the day so that he may retain a link with the degree of the non-manifestation of the Essence and not separate himself from it in all respects. For he who is swallowed up in the relational multiplicity of the Names remains a prisoner of their operations, that is [of that which, in the manifested world, appears to us as] the real multiplicity. And he is then like a one eyed man.

Thus, to the day (which is manifestation) was attributed recitation with a soft voice (which is non-manifestation) while to the night (which is non-manifestation) was attributed recitation with a loud voice (which is manifestation). As for the ritual prayers at sunset and in the evening, they are like isthmuses since they are situated between night—which we have said corresponds symbolically to the degree of the non-manifested Essence since its appearance brings about the disappearance of things—and the day, which corresponds to the degree from which the divine Names are epiphanized. It is therefore prescribed that in these two prayers recitation with a loud voice and recitation with a soft voice be joined, since the isthmus joins the two things between which it occupies this intermediate position and has a face turned toward each of them.

Beyond that, in these two prayers recitation with a loud voice should precede recitation with a soft voice. This is because the one who prays is preparing himself to receive the night, symbol of the non-manifested Essence.

This last is the principle of manifestation. But manifestation is powerful. Thus the one who prays is enjoined to confront this power with its contrary. Consequently, one recites the first two parts (*rakᶜatayn*) of the prayer with a loud voice and the others with a soft voice.

It is not the same for the prayer at sunrise (*ṣubḥ*), where the recitation is entirely in a loud voice. When it arrives, the night reabsorbs the beings in its silence, its non-manifestation, and its mystery. From then they need something which will make them come out from this mystery; which will lead them back from the world of non-manifestation to the world of manifestation and to draw them out of the silence. Thus this prayer is recited entirely in a loud voice, and it has been prescribed for us to prolong the recitation of the Koran at that time.[45]

Mawqif 271.

11

On Certitude

> *And those who follow the straight path, He increases them in guidance and brings them to piety.*
>
> (Kor. 47:17)

This means: "Those who follow the straight path" through faith and the accomplishment of pious works, "He increases them in guidance" by granting them an unveiling (*kashf*) concerning what they believe and by showing them the secret meanings of their acts of obedience. Thus it is that He also said, "Be pious toward Allāh and Allāh will teach you (Kor. 2:282)." Similarly, according to a *ḥadīth,* "He who acts in conformity to his knowledge, Allāh grants to him the knowledge which he did not yet possess." This supplementary knowledge which Allāh teaches to those who act in conformity with the knowledge which they already possess consists precisely in the unveiling of the secret of what they do. In fact, nothing is incumbent upon a legally responsible being (*mukallaf*) except, in the first place, faith; then the accomplishment of obligations—actions or abstentions—to the extent that they present themselves, respect for the prescribed limits and the firm conviction that all that is in conformity with justice. He should, in addition, abstain from reflecting on the "how" [of what is rationally incomprehensible] and avoid tendentious interpretations (*taʾwīlāt*).

To the believer who acts according to what he believes, God unveils the hidden aspect and the essential reality of things. Thus He raises him from the degree of faith—which consists in professing that the Messenger is truthful in his Message, and corresponds to [that which is designated in the Koran as] "the knowledge of certainty" (*ᶜilm al-yaqīn*, cf. Kor. 102:5)—to the degree of "the eye of certainty" (*ᶜayn al-yaqīn*, Kor. 102:7) then finally to that of "the reality of certainty" (*ḥaqq al-yaqīn*).[46] At that point, that which was only faith becomes contemplation and direct vision. This is the meaning of "being increased in guidance" and which is also called "augmentation of faith" in more than one verse and more than one *ḥadīth*. This expression is a metonymy in which the effect is designated by its cause, since it is faith, with all that it implies—words, acts, inner conviction—which is the cause of the increase of certainty and the progression up to the degrees of the "eye of certainty" and the "reality of certainty."

Conversely, infidelity and the abstention from pious works provoke a growing perdition and are the causes that hearts become "sealed" and "rusted" in conformity with the following verses: "As for those whose hearts are diseased, [the Revelation] only has the effect of increasing their impurity with a further impurity" (Kor. 9:125); "There is a disease in their hearts and Allāh augments their disease" (Kor. 2:10); "But rust has touched their hearts" (Kor. 83:14); and other analogous verses.

For him who attains certainty, there is not, properly speaking, an "increase" in the object of his vision itself. What increases is the visibility and the degree of unveiling of this object. The difference between the three certainties mentioned above consists in this: the "knowledge of certainty" requires a proof and admits of doubt; the "eye of certainty" also requires a proof[47] but it does not admit of doubt; the "reality of certainty" requires no proof and does not admit of doubt. All knowledge which is the fruit of an effective spiritual realization, that is, the knowledge which Allāh grants by His theophanies to those of his servants whom He wishes, belongs to the third category.

Thus it is clear that "increase in guidance" does not mean believing in more things but believing more in that which one already believed, and that the increase of the knowledge of the saints does not represent an increase in relation to that which Muḥammad—on him be Grace and Peace!—brought. The saints bring neither commands nor prohibitions, neither interdictions nor new laws. Simply, God unveils to them the secrets, the essential realities, the hidden senses and the esoteric meanings of that which Muḥammad brought. For every "exterior" there corresponds an "interior." The exterior of a thing is its *mulk*, the interior is its *malakūt*.[48] Allāh—may He be exalted!—said, "Thus we made Abraham see the *malakūt* of the heavens and of the earth in order that he be among those who possess certainty." (Kor. 6:75) [This verse is the scriptural proof that] the certainty that is added to faith can only be acquired by the unveiling of the esoteric reality of things and the vision of their *malakūt*.

Mawqif 222.

12

He who Speaks and he who Listens

God—may He be exalted!—said (Kor. 7:204), "When the Koran is recited"—whether it be by you yourself or by someone else who recites it for you (which would explain the passive form of the verb)[49]—"listen to him and be silent: perhaps you will receive mercy"[50]—on the condition that you listen to it as being the Voice of Allāh: for this Word is the very word of Allāh and it is He alone who speaks it, and on the condition also that he who listens be Allāh. For in every being, whether he knows it or not, Allāh is He who speaks and He who listens. When He who recites and He who listens are one, it is the same as when one speaks to oneself and when one listens to oneself.

Whoever listens to the Koran in this way obeys its injunctions, keeps himself from doing what it forbids, follows its admonitions and is attentive to the subtle allusions which it harbors. From this, the divine Mercy will be confirmed for him and will necessarily supervene in his behalf. In fact, as the scholars have said, "perhaps," when spoken by Allāh, expresses a necessary consequence.[51]

As for one who listens [to the recitation of the Koran] in some other way, he is not included in this generous promise. The divine Mercy will not be confirmed for him. If the reciter is not the listener, it could be that the latter only hears the melody, the modulations, the beauty of the voice of the reciter and does not grasp the meaning of what is said; and, all the more, he does not grasp what is beyond that meaning. And if he who listens is also the reciter, he may be one of those whom the Prophet—on him be Grace and Peace!—said: "There are many reciters of the Koran whom the Koran condemns!" God condemns the unjust, the sinners, the liars. This man is one of them. Thus, he who wishes to obtain the treasures must break the locks and seize what is beyond!

Mawqif 167.

13

On the True Fear of God

Do not fear them, but fear Me, if you are believers!

(Kor. 3:175)

Fear is of two kinds. In the first place, there is the fear of God. It is inspired by the majesty, the magnificence and the reverence which He inspires and it leaves one, according to the proverbial expression, "without gestures and without voice." It is not fear of tyranny but recognition of the divine Majesty. It is this that is experienced by the gnostics who, to various degrees—according to whether they are Messengers, prophets, angels or saints—have come to the true realization of the divine Unicity (*tawḥīd haqīqī*),[52] that is to say to precisely that which this verse prescribes. This concerns a particular *tawḥīd* [and not *tawḥīd* understood in its general sense, which consists in professing that there is but one God]: he who knows Him—may He be exalted!—also knows that He alone should be feared; for all things, in this world and in the other, are nothing more than His epiphanies and His manifestations.

Gnostics are in awe of Allāh alone, they fear (*yattaqūn*) only Him, and they protect themselves (*ittiqāʾuhum*) against Allāh only by Allāh and not by anything else.[53] This is the only effective protection, to the exclusion of any other, for one can protect oneself against a thing only by the thing itself. Thus, the lance head, the blade or the knife of steel can only be defended against by armor which is also made of steel. This is why He has said in a number of verses: "Fear Allāh"—which means "fear only Him to the exclusion of all creatures." He has also said as a form of praise: "Those who are afraid when some spirit sent by the demon touches them remember and then see clearly." (Kor. 7:201)

This concerns those who protect themselves against Allāh by Allāh, and it is because of this subtle point that the verse does not specify "against whom" they protect themselves, nor "by whom" they are protected. The beings thus described, when they perceive the coming of the satanic suggestion, which brushes them like a specter or a furtive thief, remember Allāh. It is in fact impossible for someone to be receptive to evil suggestions who remembers Allāh with presence when he is in that state of presence (*ḥuḍūr*).[54] Thus, these men "render God present" (*istaḥḍarū l-ḥaqq*) against Whom and by Whom they protect themselves. The Messenger of God has said with respect to this, "I take refuge in You against You."[55] Similarly, in the order of sensible things, he who perceives the approach of the enemy reunites (*istaḥḍara,* literally, "renders present") the equipment and the arms thanks to which he will protect himself against the enemy.

"And then they see clearly" means that they contemplate Him against Whom and by Whom they protect themselves. They flee toward Him and trust themselves totally to Him. This contemplation shelters them from the demon and his ruses and the latter returns humiliated and chagrined. He wished for their loss and, behold, he brought it about that they succeeded in making God present and in taking refuge in Him.

The second kind of fear is the fear of creatures: fear of enemies—men or jinn;[56] fear of hell, of serpents, scorpions and other torments which are found there; fear of sins and of disobedience and so on. This fear is not inspired by reverence or majesty—fear of scorpions, serpents and the like does not correspond at all to this. It is this fear which is experienced by the common believers who practice worship, renunciation and piety but for whom the veil of otherness has not been lifted from their eyes. Their hearts are always filled with that which is "other than Allāh"; they fear an "other than Allāh" in everything where God had apparently made a place of manifestation of evil and protect themselves from these creatures by other similar creatures. Against enemies, they protect themselves by fortifications and arms; against hell, its serpents and its torments they protect themselves by repentance, obedience to the Law and devotions which, in their eyes, are acts which come from themselves and belong to themselves. They fast, pray, make the pilgrimage and give alms by themselves and not by their Lord. This manner of protecting oneself is without profit. He who trusts in it is deceived and courts certain ruin.

"Do not fear them, but fear Me, if you are believers." In other words: When you are in the first station of separation,[57] in which you are still covered by a thick veil and believe with the faith of ordinary men, there is, for you, God on the one hand and, on the other hand, a creation distinct from Him possessing a contingent existence that is different from His eternal Being. Then it would be fitting for you, in order for your ordinary faith to be perfect, "to fear only Me," to the exclusion of every creature, for the creature cannot (by itself) bring you any harm or profit and there is nothing to fear or hope from it. This implies that if you are not simply one of those who believe, but one of those who sees with his own eyes and who contemplates, then one can no longer say of you that you "believe" in that which you have seen with your own eyes except in a purely metaphorical manner. In fact, "to believe" is to affirm the truthfulness of what another affirms. Now, you have passed this degree to attain that of direct vision, that in which one contemplates the effusion of the Divine reality in every existing thing—whether that thing inspires terror or not—without there being "incarnation" or "fusion." In these conditions "fear them" means "fear Me in them" for they are the places of the manifestation of My names and the particular forms of My theophanies. To each creature there corresponds a divine aspect, and it acts by this aspect, not by its sensible form. That is why he who has arrived at the perfect spiritual realization—and whose rank is thus superior to that of the simple initiate—declares that the effects are produced *in* the secondary causes—and not *by* the secondary causes.[58]

Thus when you see one of the gnostics fear a king, a tyrant, a ferocious animal or a serpent, know that in truth he does not fear the created form, which is illusory and devoid of real being, but that of which it is the epiphanic place, that is the divine Names of rigor, of vengeance and of constraining force. Between the fear of the simple believer and that of the gnostic, there is the same difference as that between a blind man and one who sees clearly.

Mawqif 131.

14

When the Sun will Rise at the Place of its Setting

The day when certain of the signs of Your Lord occur, no soul will profit from its faith.

(Kor. 6:158)[59]

According to an authentic *ḥadīth,* on that day "the sun will rise at the place of its setting." Know then that there is a veritable sun and a purely metaphorical sun. The "door of repentance" will be definitely closed the day when they both rise at the place of their setting and no soul, then, will profit from its faith.

The metaphorical sun is the star of the day, the source of sensible light. Its rising at the place of its setting and that which will follow are things known to all.

As to the veritable sun, source at the same time of sensible and spiritual light, it is referred to by the verse: "Allāh is the Light of the heavens and the earth." (Kor. 24:35)[60] Its rising at the place of its setting is the moment when it unveils itself in the place where it was hidden and obscured, that is to say in the soul, which is the veil and the occident of the sun of the essential Reality. This rising at the place of setting, that is, in the soul, is for the soul the knowledge of itself: "He who knows his soul knows his Lord."[61]

Thus the setting becomes the rising. This is the greatest sign of all. After having risen in the west, the sun of the essential Reality will never set again, since the occident which veiled and concealed it has become the very place where it rises and shines forth. Thus it will never again be obscured. As someone has said:

> The diurnal sun sets at night
> But the sun of the heart never disappears.

Then the famous "door of repentance" will be closed before him for whom the sun has risen at the place of its setting, for repentance (*tawba*) means, etymologically, return (*rujūʿ*).[62] Now for him for whom the sun of the essential Reality has risen at the place of its setting, towards whom would he return? For the divine Presence (*al-maʿiyya al-ilāhiyya*)[63] and the Infinity of the Lord are revealed to him. There is no longer a "who" to whom he can return. All the "others" are annihilated. All lights have become one. Only Allāh remains, the Unique, the Victorious, to Whom alone belongs authority. "It is to Him that you will be returned." (Kor. 2:28, 245, etc.) Now, he whose sun has risen in the west has already returned to Him in this life, without awaiting the future life. For him the Day of Resurrection has already risen. From that moment on it is imperative that he repent of his ordinary repentance, which has become, for the being who has attained this spiritual station, a fault, a sin, a mark of ignorance; for "that which is a good act for pious men is a fault for Those Who Have Drawn Near."

His faith is no longer of any use to him. In fact his faith is only useful so long as he is veiled and has not obtained direct vision and evidence. But the rising of the sun makes proofs unnecessary. When that which was hidden becomes evident, when that of which he was merely informed is directly seen, the soul no longer derives any profit from that which it believes but only from that which it contemplates and sees. The states, the intentions, the goals which he had during the phase of faith are transformed. This transformation should be understood as purely inner. As to the exterior of this being, it is not modified even an iota. He continues to behave in a way which is acceptable to the sacred Law and commendable according to customs and natural law, engaging in the activities which conform to his situation and his rank among his fellow men.

Such is the state of the gnostics when the door of knowledge is opened to them and the sun has risen for them at the place where it sets. All the rest is nothing but hypocrisy (*taṣannu*ᶜ). And it would be better for the servant, when he meets his Lord, to be covered with all the sins—polytheism excepted—than to present himself before Him with even one atom of hypocrisy.

Mawqif 172.

II

On the Unicity of Being

15

On the Supreme Identity

God (*al-ḥaqq*: the supreme Reality)—may He be exalted!—said to me, "Do you know who you are?" I replied, "Yes, I am the non-being[64] which is manifested by Your manifestation; I am the darkness which Your light illuminates."

Then He said to me, "Since you know this, persevere firmly [in this knowledge] and be careful not to claim that which does not belong to you: for the deposit (*amāna*) must be returned to its owner and the loan must be paid back. The name 'contingent being' has always belonged to you and always will belong to you."

He said to me again, "Do you know who you are?" I replied, "Yes, I am in reality God (*al-ḥaqq*). But, metaphorically and in relation to the Way, I am creature (*al-khalq*). I am a contingent being with respect to my form, but I cannot not be the necessary Being. It is the divine name *al-ḥaqq* which belongs to me by original right (*aṣl*); the name of creature is only a borrowed name and a formula of differentiation (*faṣl*). He said to me, "Veil this symbol; and let the wall fall down and bury this treasure,[65] in order that only he will be able to extract it who has put his soul through severe trials and looked his death [*rams*: literally "his tomb"] in the face."

Then God—may He be exalted!—said to me, "What are you?[66]" I replied, "I am two things, according to two different relations. With respect to You, I am the Eternal, forever and ever. I am the necessary Being who epiphanizes himself. My necessity proceeds from the necessity of Your essence and my eternity from the eternity of Your knowledge and Your attributes.

"With respect to me, I am pure non-being who has never breathed the perfume of existence, the adventitious being who remains nonexistent in his adventitiousness. I only possess being so long as I am present with You and for You. Left to myself and absent from You I am one who is not, even while he is (*fa-anā mafqūd mawjūd*)."

Then He said to me, "And who am I?" I replied, "You are the Being, necessary through Itself, alone perfect in Its essence and Its attributes. Better yet: You transcend by the perfection of Your essence the perfection of Your attributes. You are the Perfect in every state, the Transcendent with respect to everything which can come to the mind."

He replied to me: "You do not know Me!"

I said to Him without fear of being disrespectful, "You are He in Whose likeness all contingent creatures are. You are the Lord and the servant, the near and the far. You are the One and the multiple, the Sublime and the lowly, the Rich and the poor, the worshipper and the Worshipped, the contemplator and the Contemplated. In You are joined the contraries and the opposites. For You are the Apparent and the Hidden, the voyager and the sedentary, He who sows and He who cultivates. You are He who plays, who tricks and who deceives. You are the supreme Reality and I am the supreme Reality. You are creature and I am creature. You are neither this nor that and I am neither this nor that."

He said to me, "That is enough. You know Me! Hide Me from those who know Me not. For Lordship has a secret and if it were revealed, Lordship would be annihilated.[67] And servitude also has a secret and, if it were revealed, servitude would be annihilated. Praise Us for what We have taught you about Ourself: for you cannot know Us by any other than Us. Nothing leads to Us except Ourself!"

Mawqif 30.

16

The Truth which should be Concealed

If any of them says, 'I am a god apart from Him,'
We will give him Hell as a recompense.

(Kor. 21:29)

In this verse, the punishment in the future life is reserved by God for him who says, "I am a god 'apart (*min dūnihi*) from Him'" and, for it to be applicable, the "apart from Him" has to be added.[68] The creature who limits himself to saying, "I am a god" is not threatened with a punishment in a future life after God has made him contemplate the divine function (*ulūhiyya*) spreading throughout the universe just as the true Being (*al-wujūd al-ḥaqq*) spreads throughout the universe. We are dealing here, nevertheless, with a truth which ought to be concealed: for it is not good that every truth be spoken, it is not praiseworthy in every circumstance to speak the truth, nor blameworthy in every circumstance to speak falsely.

He who, in this world, declares that he is Allāh is therefore blamed. Even though it is true, it is only effectively so when, in the future life, the servant himself becomes the creator and when he can say to a thing "Be!" and it is. But, in this life, the limiting conditions proper to this lower world refute his affirmation that he is Allāh: for he has hunger and thirst, he is subject to sleep and has to go to the bathroom.

This is why, if someone says this while in full possession of his reason, the swords of both exotericism and esotericism (*suyūf al-sharīᶜa wa l-ḥaqīqa*) fall upon him and spill his blood, as happened to Hussain b. Manṣūr al-Ḥallāj—May Allāh be pleased with him!—for he had said what he said at a time when, it appears, he was fully in possession of his reason. He was therefore put to death by virtue of a juridical decision (*fatwa*) made in common by the doctors of the law and the spiritual masters, among whom were his own masters, who knew nevertheless that his words were esoterically valid.[69]

On the contrary he who says, "I am Allāh" while under the influence of a mystical intoxication and a spiritual state is not legally responsible because possession of reason is the condition of all legal responsibility, and he no longer possesses it.

Another case is that of beings like Abū Yazīd[70] who say this by virtue of a divine permission. The people of this category are protected from being harmed by creatures because of their spiritual condition.

Nor should one say, "I am He," since the sense of "I" is different from that of "He." These two terms are mutually incompatible and the identification of one with the other is therefore a pure impossibility.

As for the saying of the Prophet—on him be Grace and Peace!—which is reported in the *Ṣaḥīḥ,* where he addressed God, saying, "Make me Light!"[71]—that is to say, "Make me You!" for Allāh is the Light[72]—this was said when he was in a state which sometimes came over him but did not last.

On the other hand, one should not say, "I am other than Him." This is an empty statement, since, by definition, the Creator [as such] is other than the creature. It is as though one said, "Water is not fire" or "The heaven is not the earth." Rather, observe what comes to you from Him. If He says to you, "I am you, and you are Me," listen and be silent! And if He says to you, "You are other than Me and I am other than you," listen and conform yourself to that. . . .

Mawqif 322.

17

On the Eternal Solitude of the Divine Essence

We have created every thing according to a measure.

(Kor. 54:49)

(According to one reading which is not very widespread, that of Ibn Sammāk, *kullu* ["every"] is considered to be in the nominative [rather than the accusative *kulla*, which is the usual reading].)[73]

Know that there is not a divine Essence on the one hand; and, on the other, essences proper to creatures which are independent and subsist by themselves upon whom He has not conferred Being. There is nothing other than the divine Essence. It is this divine Essence which, without multiplying or dividing, is the essence of creatures; and, reciprocally, the essences of creatures are identical to the divine Essence. This does not mean that God has His essence and that creatures also have their own essences and that the divine Essence unites itself with them, or mixes with them, or infuses itself in them. All these things are impossible and that is not at all what I wish to say.

Rather, I mean that His essence—may He be exalted!—that is, His very being, through which creatures subsist and which rules them, is the essence of the creatures. In other words, when one speaks of the "essences of creatures" it is only a manner of expressing the manifestation of the true Being, when He clothes Himself in the properties which are implied by the predispositions of creatures; that is to say their immutable prototypes (*aᶜyānuha al-thābita*) as they are in the divine science, non-existent, for ever and ever, being nothing but pure aspects or relationships in the heart of the divine Reality and having no being of their own.[74]

But just as it is the hidden which has authority over the apparent and the non-manifested which acts upon the manifested, it is the determining properties conferred by the predispositions [of the prototypes], immutably contained in the divine knowledge, but devoid of being, which have authority over the true Being, which epiphanizes itself in conformity to these properties. Thus, although these predispositions are in truth non-existent, the properties and attributes [which condition His manifestation] are theirs, but in Him [since He alone is].

His essence—may He be exalted!—is the true Being, eternal, self-subsistent. The essences of creatures are all identical to the true Being, in so far as He manifests Himself in the states implied by the prototypes, which are adventitious with respect to manifestation, and immutable with respect to the divine Knowledge.

Thus it is He—may He be exalted!—who is our essence insofar as it manifests the attributes of our immutable prototypes. But our states have authority over Him insofar as He is qualified by them. We are His essence insofar as He manifests Himself through us. For He only manifests Himself through us even though we are pure non-being. Now the essence of a thing is that by which it manifests itself. The fact that we speak of "Him" and of "us" does not bring what we have just said into question. The need to make ourselves understood imposes that, but there is only one single Essence, or one single Reality, which we call "God" when it manifests itself in an active mode, when it produces effects and is endowed with the attributes of perfection, and which we call "creature" or "servant" when it manifests itself in a passive mode, when it is receptive and endowed with the attributes of imperfection. But in either case it is the same thing.

It is the same for the attributes (*ṣifāt*): creatures do not possess attributes different from the divine attributes. The attributes which, with respect to Him, are infinite and operate on all the objects on which it is proper for them to operate and which, with respect to us, are limited and only operate upon a portion of these objects, are identical. For example, His absolute power is exercised on all possible things, while His power, insofar as it is conditioned by us, is only exercised on a portion of them.

In the same way, His absolute knowledge embraces at the same time the impossible, the necessary, and the possible whereas His knowledge, insofar as it is conditioned by us and is attributed to us, only embraces a part of the knowable things to the exclusion of others. These same attributes are divine to the extent that they are absolute, and creatural to the extent that they are conditioned. But, in either of these states, in either of these relations, they are identical and are only distinguished by their character of being absolute or conditioned. The absolute is the same as that which appears in the manifested world as conditioned, even if it is different from it from the point of view and comprehension [of creatures]. Limitation and adventitiousness only characterize the attributes to the extent that they are in relation with creatures.

Analogously, the acts of the creatures are His acts—may He be exalted!—and His acts are the acts of the creatures. It is for this reason that, in the Book and the Sunna, the acts are attributed sometimes to God alone, sometimes to creatures alone, sometimes to God through the mediation of creatures, and sometimes to creatures through the mediation of God.[75] Understand!

O! you who read this, take care not to accuse us of professing incarnationism, the union [of God with the creature], atheism or heresy. For we do not take responsibility for your misunderstanding and foolishness.

Mawqif 64.

18

Being and Non-being

Surely, We have created each thing according to a measure

(Koran 54:49)

According to the reading of Ibn Sammāk, the word *kull* (each) should be pronounced in the nominative, *kullu* [and not in the accusative—*kulla*—as the usual reading has it. As a consequence the first three Arabic words of the verse could then be translated as "Surely, We are each thing," the pronoun "We" referring always to God].

Allāh—May He be exalted!—teaches us through this that He is each thing with respect to its essence, whether that thing is existent or not. For the notion of 'thing' is the most universal of all and applies to all that can be known or spoken of. Allāh is in Himself the non-being and the being, the inexistent and the existent. He is at the same time that which we designate by 'absolute non-being and by 'absolute being'; or by 'relative non-being' and 'relative being.' A certain thing, which was inexistent, has come into existence. Another thing will never come into existence. The first is non-being in a certain relation, and the other is non-being in all relations. And so it is with all things. Now, all these designations come back to God alone, for there is nothing which we can perceive, know, write or say which is not Him. Existence is not something which is added to the existent thing, nor is inexistence something which is added to the inexistent thing.

His light[76] spreads out and this operation expresses nothing other than the ordered unfolding of His attributes over the non-being. What is called "the possibles" are those things which show themselves capable of receiving that light and those which are called "the impossibles" are those which are unable to receive the light. It is to just this that the Prophet—upon Him be Grace and Peace!—alluded when He said, "Allāh created the creatures in the darkness, then He sprinkled them with His light. Those who were touched by some of this light are on the good way; and those who failed to be touched by it are astray."

He is the light which unfolds and the non-being upon which it unfolds. That of the non-being which receives the light is not other than His essence: for it is the very material of the non-being. In the divine knowledge, everything which is possesses the forms which are called "the immutable prototypes" (*al-aᶜyān al-thābita*); and that which has not received the light is lost in the non-being, which is the Darkness of the divine Essence. The things which have been existentiated and then have disappeared are the forms and the accidents. As for the substances, once they have come into existence, they will never return to the non-being.

Mawqif 287.

19

And He is with you wherever you are . . .

And He is with you wherever you are . . .

(Kor. 57:4)

Know that the pronoun "He" (*Huwa*) has as its function, according to the principles of the organization of the language, the representation of the non-manifested (*ghayb*).[77] This non-manifested can eventually become manifested at a given moment in a given state. But here, *huwa* represents the occultation of the divine Essence, which can in no instance manifest itself to any creature whatsoever or in any state whatsoever, in this world or in the other. Thus it concerns the absolutely Non-Manifested, which transcends all allusion (*ishāra*), for one can indicate by an allusion only something which is situated somewhere. The absolutely Non-Manifested cannot be designated by any expression (*ᶜibāra*) which could limit It, separate It, or include It. In spite of this, every allusion alludes only to Him, every designation designates Him, and He is at the same time the Non-Manifested and the Manifested.

"To be with" (*al-maᶜiyya*), is used according to the rules of the language, when there is a companionship of two things possessing an independent existence; as for example in the phrase "Zayd is with ᶜAmr." By contrast, one does not say "to be with" in the case of a substance and an accident, for an accident does not have an autonomous existence since it subsists only through the substance of which it is an inherent attribute: its definition is to be that which, if it exists, exists only in a subject (*mawdūᶜ*). Thus one would not say, "Zayd is with the whiteness or with the movement." Similarly, one would not say, "The knowledge of Zayd is with him."

In the verse we are commenting on, the companionship expressed by "with" is that of the Being and the non-being, for there is no Being other than Allāh. The most truthful words ever spoken by a poet are these:

> Is not everything outside of Allāh illusion?[78]

That which is illusion is pure non-being, and if we attribute being to anything other than the divine Reality (*al-Ḥaqq*) it is in a metaphorical way, since it is only an imaginary existence. Being belongs properly only to Him—May He be exalted!—and it is legitimate to deny it to everything which is not Him as is normal when dealing with purely metaphorical relations.[79]

If Allāh—May He be exalted!—was not, by His very Essence,[80] which is the Being of all that is, 'with' the creatures, we could not attribute being to any of these creatures and they could not be perceived either by the senses, by the imagination, or by the intellect. It is their 'being with' which assures to creatures a relation with Being. Better yet, it is their being itself. This 'being with' embraces all things, whether they are sublime or lowly, great or small. It is through it that they subsist. He is the pure Being by which 'that which is' is. The 'being with' of Allāh consists, therefore, in the fact that He is with us through His essence; that is, through that which we call the divine Self (*huwiyya*), universally present although we cannot speak of it as "diffusion" (*sarayān*), "inherency" (*ḥulūl*), "union" (*ittiḥād*), "mixture" (*imtizāj*) or "solution" (*inḥilāl*).[81] These words cannot in fact be used unless one is dealing with two distinct realities, corresponding to the common belief. But there is for us only one unique, eternal Reality whose transcendence precludes that contingent things be present in themselves or that It be present in the contingent things.

As for those who maintain, according to the most widespread opinion, that Allāh—May He be exalted!—is "with us" by His knowledge [and not by His essence], if they mean by that to preserve the divine Essence from the company of creatures, we know, in fact, that the transcendence which certainly belongs to the Essence belongs equally, by right, to the divine attributes.[82] And if they wish to say that the Essence is one and indivisible while the creatures are multiple, this objection applies in the same way to the divine Knowledge which is also a single and indivisible reality. He who pretends to possess a knowledge, when he is ignorant even of the means by which it is acquired, is ignorant *a fortiori* of that which he pretends to know.

When you hear a gnostic say, or when you read in his writings, that "Allāh is with the things through His knowledge," know that he does not understand that in the same way as the simple theologians. He means something else, but the expression of it is veiled because of those who contradict and make trouble. According to the master of the gnostics, Muḥyī l-Dīn [Ibn ᶜArabī], "to say that Allāh is with all things through His knowledge is in conformity with usual practice (*adab*), while to say that He is with all things through His essence is more in conformity with what spiritual realization (*taḥqīq*) teaches." "Usual practice" in this case means "when one is speaking to those who are under the veils [of ignorance], taking into account their pretensions," or in a more general way, that not every truth should be told and it is not right to divulge everything that one knows.

Indications of this divine 'being with' are contained in the following verses: "And He is witness of all things" (Kor. 34:47); "And Allāh, behind them, encompasses them" (Kor. 85:20); "Wherever you turn, there is the Face of Allāh" (Kor. 2:116). The word "Face" (*wajh*) means here the Essence. *Wajh* is in fact one of the ways of designating the essence of a being, and the very wording of the verse furnishes a support for our interpretation and rules out any contrary interpretation, for in current speech, "Zayd came in person" can be expressed equally well as *nafsuhu* (literally, "his soul"), *wajhuhu* (literally, "his face") or *ᶜaynuhu* (literally, "his being" or "his essence").[83]

There is, on the other hand, a special manner for Allāh to "be with" the elite of the simple believers. It consists in the concomitance of His grace (*imdād*) with noble virtues and excellence of character. The following verses testify to this: "In truth, Allāh is with those who fear him and those who do good" (Kor. 16:128); "In truth, Allāh is with those who are patient" (Kor. 2:153; 8:47); or further, this saying of the Prophet—on him be Grace and Peace!—"In truth, Allāh is with the judge so long as he does not depart from justice"; as well as other similar sayings from divine or prophetic sources. All this concerns the manifestation in certain creatures, but not in others, of some of the perfections of the Being.

Finally there is for Allāh a particular manner of 'being with' the elite of the elite, that is, with the Messengers, the prophets, and with their spiritual heirs—may Allāh grant His Grace and his Peace to all of them! This is nothing other than the predominance of the status of the necessary and eternal Being over the status of the contingent and adventitious creature that is deprived of real essence. Thus He says, speaking to Mūsā (Moses) and Hārūn (Aaron), "Surely, with the two of you, I hear and I see" (Kor. 20:40), which means "through the two of you I hear and through the two of you I see, for My company has subjugated your two beings. There is nothing here but Me, there is no more 'you' except with respect to the apparent form." This spiritual station is known among initiates—may Allāh be pleased with them!—by the name of "Proximity through obligatory works" (*qurb al-farāʾiḍ*)[84] and consists in the manifestation of the Lord and the occultation of the servant. When one addresses someone who has attained this station, it is God who responds in his place, "Here am I!"

This station is superior to the one called "Proximity through supererogatory works" (*qurb al-nawāfil*). If someone finds himself in this latter station, when someone says "O Allāh!" he, on the contrary, will respond in place of Allāh, "Here I am."

That Allāh is "with" all things is a certainty. Nonetheless, one cannot say of something that it is "with Him." For, while there is an explicit scriptural basis (*naṣṣ*) in the first case, the correlative affirmation that all things are with Him is only implicit.

It follows certainly from the fact that someone is with you, that you are with him. But we cannot, in the absence of scriptural support, affirm "I am with Him."

Mawqif 132.

20

The Exclusive Orientation

We say: O fire, be coolness and peace for Abraham.

(Kor. 21:69)[85]

The fire is that of the natural constitution and represents the demands of the animal soul, and it is ordered [by God] to be "coolness and peace" for Abraham. Now Abraham does not designate in reality an individual but a collective personality, since for every collective reality there corresponds a being who symbolizes it, as Adam symbolizes humanity. It is for this reason that God said, "Certainly Abraham was a community." (Kor. 16:20)

Abraham represents the totality of those who follow his way, since he is their origin and their father. He symbolizes the most pure recognition of the divine unicity, the exclusive orientation towards the Lord of the worlds,[86] just as Adam is the origin and the father of the human race, that is to say, of animals endowed with reason. Muḥammad—On him be Grace and Peace!—is the father and origin of Abraham and Adam[87] endowing them with that which constitutes their paternity. Whoever follows the religion of Abraham *is* Abraham.[87bis] Thus the fire is ordered to be "coolness and peace" for Abraham and those who follow his religion, those who are characterized by the divine Saying: "O my people, I disavow all that you associate [with God]. I orient my face with an exclusive orientation towards Him, who created the heavens and the earth and I am not one of the associators." (Kor. 6:78–79) "I separate myself from you and from that which you invoke alongside of Allāh." (Kor. 19:48).

God has prescribed that we follow the religion of Abraham with His saying: "Follow the religion of Abraham in the most pure way—and he was not one of the associators" (Kor. 3:95); "And who is more perfect in his religion than he who submits his face to Allāh, does good and follows the religion of Abraham in the most pure way?" (Kor. 4:125)

Abraham attributed to God alone, without division, being and everything which flows from it (*al-wujūd wa tawabiᶜ al-wujūd*). As a consequence, he who attributes to something other than Him—may He be exalted!—a "being," eternal or not, distinct from Him, is not among those who follow the religion of Abraham. Thus he is not Abraham, and the fire has not received, with respect to him, the order to be "coolness and peace." On the contrary, he is among those who separated from the religion of Abraham and have gone to their ruin, in conformity with the divine Saying: "Who therefore, if he is not a fool, separates himself from the religion of Abraham?" (Kor. 2:130)

Mawqif 183.

21

Concerning Universal Life

And, from water We have made every living thing.

(Kor. 21:30)

God informs us that, through His will and His power, He has "made" every living thing out of water. "To make" signifies here "to make something come to be"; "to form." In other words He has made the water take a form that it did not have. It is for this reason that He attributes two complements to the verb,[88] for by 'thing' we must understand here only the form of the thing, not its spirit, which proceeds from the Breath of the Most-Merciful (*nafas al-Raḥmān*).[89] On the other hand, the word "thing" means "that which is existent" (*mawjūd*), to the exclusion of that which is non-existent (*maᶜdūm*), for one cannot give form to non-being.

Thus every living thing proceeds from water. Now everything is living, for everything praises God and something is able to praise only if it is living and knows *whom* he praises and *through whom* he praises. "There is not a thing which does not glorify Him through His praise." (Kor. 17:44)[90] Therefore it is evident that life is coextensive with existence. Every existent is living with a life which conforms to the predisposition which is implied by its form and its ontological degree. The accidents themselves have a life which conforms to their predispositions since they are existent: in fact, an accident is properly something which, if it exists, exists in a substance.[91] Thus accidents themselves also live an autonomous life, distinct from that of the substances in which they exist.

It is the same for forms, appearances, words and acts, as is stated in an authentic tradition according to which [after death] the acts will clothe themselves in forms and confront the one who accomplished them, putting him at ease in his tomb if the acts were pious and making him miserable if the acts were evil.[92]

Although this life is one—for it is nothing other than the life of Allāh, through which all things are living—it manifests itself in varying modalities and diversifies itself according to the receptivity of the forms which receive it. The life of that which we call "accident" is different from the life of that which we call "substance," which is different from the life of that which we call "mineral," "vegetable," "animal" or "man." But there is nothing in the universe that is not living although in certain cases the life may be hidden while in other cases it is manifested.

Know that this "water" from which God made every living thing is not the water perceptible by the senses—which is one of the four elements and whose characteristic qualities are coldness and humidity—but the water of the river of life of primordial Nature, which is situated above the elements. According to a prophetic tradition, it is into this river that Jibrīl—upon him be Peace!—plunges every day, after which he shakes himself off and from each drop of water God creates an angel. Also, as is reported in the *Ṣaḥīḥ* of Bukhārī, those whom intercession has enabled to emerge from the fires of hell will be submerged in this same river in such a way that they will "spring up again."[93] It is also this river which is spoken of in the tradition according to which the first thing that Allāh created was a precious stone which He gazed upon with the eye of His majesty. The stone melted from shame when it became aware of His gaze and became a water in which are hidden all the jewels and all the pearls of His knowledge.[94] There exist different versions of this tradition all of which refer to the Muhammadan Reality,[95] which is the *Materia prima* of the universe, the Reality of realities, the substance of everything which is "other than Allāh."

Seen in this light, sensible water, just like the other elements, is one of the forms of the "water" mentioned in this verse. The ensemble of the four elements, considered with respect to the intelligible content (*maᶜānī*) of their forms, constitutes the supreme Nature, that is, the "water" from which all living things are made and which is present in each of the four sensible elements. Thus in the element "fire" is found water, fire, air and earth; in the element "water," fire, water, air and earth, and so on[96] . . .

Mawqif 325.

22

The Secrets of the Lām-Alif

These symbols we make for men but they will only be understood by those who know.

(Kor. 29:43)

Know that God proposes symbols by His acts as well as by His works, for the purpose of a symbol is to lead to understanding, in such a way that the intelligible object becomes as evident as the sensible object [which symbolizes it]. Among the symbols which He proposes by His acts is the creation of the letters of the alphabet. Their lines contain, in fact, secrets which only one endowed with knowledge and wisdom can grasp. Among all these letters is found the *Lām-Alif,* which conceals subtle allusions, secrets and innumerable enigmas, and a teaching.[97]

Among these secrets is the fact that the combination of the two letters *Lām* and *Alif* [in the *Lām-Alif*] is analogous to the combination of the divine Reality with the forms of the creatures. From a certain point of view these are two distinct letters and, from another point of view, one single letter. In the same way, the divine Reality[98] and the forms of the creatures are two distinct things from a certain point of view and one and the same thing from another point of view.

There is also the fact that we do not know which of the two branches [of the *Lām-Alif*] is the *Alif* and which is the *Lām*. If you say, "It is the *Lam* which is the first branch" you are right. If you say, "It is the *Alif*" you are also right. If you say that you are incapable of deciding between one or the other, then you are right again.

In the same way, if you say that only the divine Reality manifests itself and that the creatures are non-manifest, you speak the truth. If you say the opposite you also speak the truth. And if you confess your perplexity on this subject, you speak the truth again.

Among the secrets of the *Lām-Alif*, there is also this: God and the creature are two names which in fact designate one and the same Named, which is the divine Essence which manifests Itself through both. In the same way the *Lām* and the *Alif* are two designations which apply to one and the same "named" for they constitute the double name of the single letter.

Another secret: just as the form of the letter which is called the *Lām-Alif* cannot be manifested by one of the letters which constitute it independently of the other, so also it is impossible that the divine Reality or the creation manifest independently of each other. God without the creation is non-manifested and the creation without God is deprived of being.

Another secret: the two branches of the *Lām-Alif* unite and separate. In the same way God and the creatures are indiscernible with respect to the essential reality and are distinct with respect to their ontological degree, for the ontological degree of the creator God is not the same as that of the created servant.

Another secret resides in the fact that the writer, when he writes the "*Lām-Alif*," sometimes begins by writing the branch which appears first in the completed form of the *Lām-Alif*, and sometimes in that which appears second. So it goes with the knowledge of God and the creation: sometimes the knowledge of the creation precedes knowledge of God—this is the way referred to by the formula, "He who knows his soul knows his Lord."[98bis] This is the way of the "itinerants" (*al-sālikūn*); on the contrary, sometimes the knowledge of Allāh precedes the knowledge of the creation. This is the way of election and divine attraction (*jadhb*), that is to say, the way of the "desired" (*al-murādūn*).[99]

Another secret is that [when the *Lām-Alif* is pronounced] the ordinary perception grasps only the sound *Lā*, which is the named, although there are two letters, the *Lām* and the *Alif*. In the same way ordinary perception does not distinguish the two "names"—"God"[100] and "creation"—[which inseparably constitute the total Reality] although they are in fact two distinct things.

Another secret is that when the *Lām* and the *Alif* combine to form the *Lām-Alif* each hides the other. Similarly, the divine Reality, when it "combines" with the creatures in a strictly conceptual mode (*tarkīban maʿnawiyyan*), is hidden to the eyes of the spiritually veiled, who see only the creatures. Conversely, it is the creatures that disappear in the eyes of the masters of the Unicity of contemplation (*waḥdat al-shuhūd*),[101] for they see only God alone. Thus, both God and the creatures hide the other [as the *Lām* and the *Alif*] but from two different points of view.

Among the secrets of the *Lām-Alif* there is also this: when the two branches, the *Lām* and the *Alif*, merge together, with the result that the form *Lā* disappears to the eye of the observer, the significance attached to this form disappears also. In the same way, when there is the state of extinction (*fanāʾ*)—which the men of the way also call "union" (*ittiḥād*)[102]—the worshipper and the Worshipped, the Lord and the servant, disappear together. If there is no worshipper, there is no Worshipped; and if there is no servant, there is no Lord. For, when two terms are correlative, the disappearance of one necessarily brings about the disappearance of the other, and therefore they disappear together.

It is for you to pursue these analogies, and to discover what they teach!

Mawqif 215.

III

The Theophanies

23

The Face of God

Turn your face toward the sacred Mosque.

(Kor. 2:144,149,150)

This means: "Turn the [divine] face which is particular to you"—of which God has said, "Only the Face of your Lord subsists." (Kor. 55:27)[103]

This face is the secret (*sirr*)[104] through which your spirit subsists, just as your body only subsists through your spirit. It is the source of man's being and the command [formulated in the verse] is in reality concerned with this. God, in fact, does not consider your exterior form but only your heart—which is the "divine face" proper to each of you, and it is this "divine face" which, in you, "contains" God even though His sky and His earth cannot contain Him.[105] When God commands that we turn toward the *qibla*,[106] He intends that it should be this face which turns. Only through it do we hear and see. He who turns [toward the *qibla*] with his body alone, without also turning this face, has not truly turned. He who looks only with his eyes of flesh, without looking with this face also, does not truly look. Thus God has said, "You will see those [the infidels] who look at you but do not see you at all." (Kor. 7:198) This is because they look only with their bodily vision and not with the "face" particular to them, their "secret." Similarly, one who listens only with his bodily hearing independently of this face, does not hear. That is why God said, "They have ears but they hear not." (Kor. 7:179)

He who turns [toward God] only with this conical organ which is his heart of flesh does not grasp or understand, "They have a heart but they do not understand." (Kor. 7:179)

He who looks with his finite eye only sees finite things—bodies, colors or surfaces. He who looks with the eye of his hidden spirit sees the hidden things—spiritual beings, forms of the world of the absolute Imagination, jinns—all of which are still only created beings and therefore veils. But he who looks with his face, that is to say, his secret (*sirr*), sees the face which God has in each thing; for, in truth, only Allāh sees Allāh, only Allāh knows Allāh.

These three "eyes" are in reality only one and are only distinguished by the difference of their objects of perception. How surprising and disconcerting! He who looks cannot himself make the distinction between the look of his bodily eyes, that of his spirit and that of his "secret"—that is to say of his particular "face"—except by the nature of that which he perceives!

It is this "face" that the saying of God refers to: "O son of Adam, I was sick and you did not visit Me. I was hungry and you did not feed Me, I was thirsty and you did not give Me to drink . . ."[107]

Further, it is this that is referred to in the *ḥadīth,* "I am his hearing . . . his look . . ." where God enumerates successively all the faculties of the servant.[108] It is also because of it that God said, "And your Lord has decreed that you should worship none but Him," (Kor. 17:23)[109] for in reality it is this divine face alone which is worshipped in every creature—fire, sun, star, animal or angel. The consideration of this face is necessary in every act, religious or not.

When [the gnostic] turns toward the *qibla* to accomplish the ritual prayer, he sees that he who turns is God and that that toward which he turns is also God. When he gives alms, he sees that he who gives is God and that he who receives is also God, as is said in the verse: "Do they not know that it is Allah himself who accepts the repentance of His servants and who receives the alms?" (Kor. 9:104) It is also reported in the *Ṣaḥīḥ* that the alms fall first of all in the Hand of the All-Merciful [before falling in the hand of him for whom it is intended].

When he recites the Koran, he sees that he who speaks is God, and that he to whom is spoken is God also. When he hears the Koran, he sees that the Speech is God and that the hearer is God. When he looks at anything whatever, he sees that he who looks is God and that which is looked at is God.

For he sees God through God—but be careful not to believe that this is a matter of incarnation, union, infusion or generation.[110] I disavow all of that. As the Shaikh al-Akbar said:

> We have left behind us the agitated seas
> How can men know where we are going?

As for the "sacred Mosque" [mentioned in the introductory verse], although this term applies literally to the Mosque perceived by the senses, it should be understood as designating the degree which totalizes all the divine Names, that is to say the degree of the divinity (*ulūhiyya*), which is the "place of the prostration"[111]—of the prostration of the heart, not of the body. One of the Masters was asked, "Does the heart prostrate itself?" He replied, "[Yes] and it will never arise from this prostration!"[112] The word "sacred" (*ḥarām*) means that a heart which has not disengaged itself from the sphere of the soul and the sphere of created beings is forbidden to penetrate into this place. [The continuation of the verse:] "Wherever you are, turn your face" [toward the sacred Mosque] means, "Wherever you are, in the accomplishment of works of worship or in the ordinary acts of life, contemplate Him—in what you eat, in what you drink, in him or her whom you marry, always knowing that He is at once the Contemplator and the Contemplated:

> He swore *by the Contemplator and the Contemplated*[113]
> In so doing, He swore only by Himself, not by any other than Him.

Mawqif 149.

24

Transcendence and Immanence

On that day, We will display Gehenna to the infidels, those whose eyes were covered with a veil which kept them from the remembrance of Me, and who could not hear.

(Kor. 18:100–101)

This is both a warning and a threat. For each being, Gehenna is in accordance with his state and his station. "Gehenna" means, according to its etymology, "distancing." For some, Gehenna will consist in being deprived of the divine vision; for others it will consist, in addition to this privation, in punishment as well.

As to infidelity (*kufr*), it can be either manifest or secret. There is a reference in the *Ṣaḥīḥ* of Bukhārī to "an infidelity beneath an infidelity."[114]

Infidelity properly consists, according to its etymology, in *hiding*,[115] and it is for this reason that one who sows seed is also called *kāfir*. Manifest infidelity consists in the fact of hiding and denying the message of the prophets of God. This is infidelity in the ordinary sense of the term. As to secret infidelity, which is more difficult to perceive than the tiniest ant, it consists in "hiding" the true, necessary and eternal Being, from whom the heavens, the earth and that which is between them draw all their reality, by attributing to contingent things that which belongs only to Him; that is, in attributing to them a being distinct from the true Being.

"Those whose eyes were covered with a veil which kept them from a remembrance of Me" refers to those whose eyes were covered with a veil which prevented them from seeing Me and therefore from remembering My presence, whether at the time of seeing the created forms, their contours and their colors, or before seeing them, or after seeing them.[116]

"And who could not hear" refers to those who were incapable of hearing as coming from Me that which they heard coming from the mouth of creatures, even though I am in truth He who speaks (*al-mutakallim*) hidden behind the wall of every created form. Consider the case of Moses—Upon him be Peace! When he heard the call coming from the burning bush, he knew that it was Allāh who spoke, even though the bush was located in a very precise direction in space, whereas God is not in any direction in space!

If they are incapable of seeing God in the forms through which He manifests Himself and the particular determinations which He takes upon Himself, if their eyes are covered with a veil which prevents them from remembering Him at the very moment when they perceive the manifested forms, if they are unable to hear His word, all this is because of their exclusive attachment to the divine transcendence (*tanzīh*) as it is conceived by their intellects, without letting this transcendence be mitigated by the immanence (*tashbīh*) which is inseparable from it in the sacred Law.[117] They have not known that Allāh is infinitely transcendent and exalted above all inherence, above all union and above all mixture with the creature, at the very moment when, with regard to His name the Apparent (*al-ẓāhir*),[118] He manifests Himself in the forms and is thus apprehended by all the senses, perceived by every organ of perception, internal or external. It is He who is heard by the sense of hearing, He who is touched by the sense of touch, for He who manifests Himself is the very essence of that which manifests Him. The Imām of the gnostics, the Shaikh Muḥyī l-Dīn said:

If you say that God transcends you,
Your sacred Law affirms that He is nonetheless
within the reach of your hand
And yet it also affirms His transcendence.
Be conscious of both this and that
In spite of the weakness of your intellect!

This is why one can describe Him by the attributes of contingent beings and ascribe to Him their conditions. This is the explanation of the Saying of the Lord (*al-ḥadīth al-rabbānī*) reported in the *Ṣaḥīḥ*: "I was sick and you did not visit Me, I was hungry and you did not feed Me . . . ";[119] and in the verse: "In truth, those who make a pact with you, make a pact with Allāh Himself, and the Hand of Allāh is above their hands." (Kor. 18:10)[120]

Similarly, He may be named by the names of all the contingent beings, as is shown by the verse: "It is not you who threw when you threw, but it is Allāh Himself who threw" (Kor. 8:17)[121]

Abū Saᶜīd al-Kharrāz said: "I have never known Allāh—May He be exalted!—except through the coincidence in Him of the opposites." Then he recited: "He is the First and the Last, the Apparent and the Hidden." (Kor. 57:3)

When one names "Abū Saᶜīd al-Kharrāz" it is He that one names.[122] Each time that expressions are found in the Koran or the Sunna that imply His immanence, they correspond to the degree of His manifestation and His determination by the forms which manifest Him by virtue of His name "the Apparent." Each time that expressions of His transcendence are found, they correspond to the degree of His withdrawal from the forms by virtue of His name "the Hidden" [...].[123]

Mawqif 193.

25

The Light of the Heavens and of the Earth

> *Allāh is the Light of the heavens and of the earth. His light is like a niche in which is found a lamp. This lamp is in a glass. This glass is like a shining star. It draws its flame from a blessed tree, an olive tree which is neither of the east nor of the west. The oil nearly shines of itself without even being touched by the fire. Light upon light. Allāh guides towards His light whom He wills. Allāh makes symbols for men and Allāh knows all things.*
>
> (Kor. 24:35)[124]

In this precious verse, He teaches us that, with regard to His name *al-Nūr* (The light),[125] Allāh—the Name which totalizes all the Names—is the Light of the heavens and of the earth, that is to say, of their very being, and that it is by Him that they subsist and by Him that they are manifested. In fact, it is by the light that what was sealed in the Darkness of the non-being appeared. If it were not for His light, nothing would be perceived and there would be no difference between a shadow and that which projects it. The light is the cause (*sabab*) of the manifestation of creatures—among whom are the earth and the heavens—just as is the case in the physical world where the darkness of night makes things as if inexistent in relation to the observer until the moment when the appearance of the light brings about the appearance of the things and distinguishes them from each other. This is true to such an extent that one of the philosophers even said that colors were inexistent in the dark and that light was a condition *sine qua non* of their existence.

If God has honored the heavens and the earth by mentioning them in this verse, it is because heaven is the place of the pure spirits (*ruḥāniyyat*) and earth is the symbolic place of the beings endowed with a body. Both of them are illuminated by one unique Light without its being separated, divided or partitioned.

The absolute Light cannot be perceived any more than absolute Darkness can. Thus the light has shone on the darkness in such a way that the darkness is perceived through the light and the light through the darkness. This is the sense of this saying of the masters: "God manifests Himself through the creatures, and the creatures manifest themselves through Him." As the Shaikh al-Akbar said:

If He were not, if we were not,
That which is would not be.

In other words, without God the creatures would not be existentiated (*khalqun bi-lā ḥaqqin lā yūjad*) and without the creature, God would not be manifested (*ḥaqqun bi-lā khalqin lā yaẓhar*). Know however that God, in order to manifest Himself by His essence to His essence, has no need of creatures since, with relation to Essence, he is absolutely independent with respect to worlds and even with respect to His own names. For from this point of view, to whom would He name Himself? To whom could He describe Himself? At this degree, there is only the one and absolute Essence! On the other hand, when He manifests Himself with His names and His attributes—which implies the manifestation of the effects—He needs (*huwa muftaqir*) the creatures.[126] The Shaikh al-Akbar alluded to this in these verses:

Each of them is in need
Neither of them can do without the other

"Them" here means God and the creature. This dependence of the divine Names with respect to the beings who are their places of manifestation is not an imperfection. On the contrary, it constitutes perfection on the level of the Names and the Attributes since the need which the cause has of its effect represents perfection itself. This relation is in fact necessary in order that the divine Names, which are only distinguished by their effects, can be distinguished from one another. At the same time, the divine Names, by the one of their "faces" which is turned toward the Essence, are themselves totally autonomous with respect to worlds. In this respect, they are nothing other than the Essence itself and that is why each of them can be qualified and designated by all of the other Names in the same way as the Essence.[127]

In one of my contemplative visions, I saw the following: an immense open register was presented to me. On each line a divine Name was written and then was successively qualified on the same line by all the other Names. On the following line another Name was written and similarly qualified by all the others and it continued like that until the list of the ninety-nine divine Names had been exhausted.

On the other hand, if one considers the "face" of the Names which is turned toward the created worlds, they are, from this point of view, dependent on these created worlds to the extent that they search to produce their effects: the one who searches is dependent with respect to that for which he searches.

The heavens, the earth and the creatures, whose light is the Name *al-nūr*, are the shadows of the Names and the Attributes projected upon the immutable prototypes fixed in the divine Knowledge (*al-aʿyān al-thābita fī l-ḥaḍrat al-ʿilmiyya*).[128] In fact every shadow has need of a surface such as the earth or water upon which it can project itself. It is light which renders the shadow visible, but it is the vertical object [illuminated by this light] which gives it its form. In this case, the vertical object corresponds to the degree of the Names and the Attributes, and the Light is the Being which spreads itself over the possibles.

Then God responded [in the verses which follow] to the question: Did the illumination of the earth, the heavens and all the creatures produce itself directly or through an intermediary? Should it be understood as a conjunction, a union or a mixture? By recourse to the symbol of the niche, the glass and the lamp, He lets us know that this illumination operates without union, mixture or conjunction through the intermediary of the Muhammadan Reality (*al-haqīqa al-muḥammadiyya*), which is the first determination (*al-taʿayyun al-awwal*), the Isthmus of Isthmuses (*barzakh al-barāzikh*),[129] the place of the theophany of the Essence and the appearance of the Light of lights. It is this Muhammadan Reality which is designated by the "glass." As for the "niche," it represents the totality of creatures—with the exception of the Muhammadan Reality, for it is from the "glass" and by its mediation that the light is perpetually spread. As for the "lamp," it symbolizes the existential and relative light (*al-nūr al-wujūdī al-iḍāfī*) [. . .].[130]

Next, God informs us that this glass, through which light reaches the niche, possesses this fineness, this plenitude, this purity, this aptitude to receive the light and spread it through the niche because of its perfect and unsurpassable predisposition, to the point where one can say that the following distich of Ṣāḥib Ibn ʿAbbād[131] applies to it:

> The cup was so pure and the wine so clear that they became similar, to the point where one did not know
>
> Whether there was wine without a cup or a cup without wine.

This is the meaning of "like a shining star."

It draws its flame—here it is a matter of the lamp, that is to say, the relative existential light. "From a tree": from a principal, from a source. *Blesses*—its benediction is perennial and its superabundance inexhaustible. *Neither from the east nor the west*—we cannot say of this tree, from which the lamp draws its flame, either that it is "oriental"—which would connect it with the rising of the sun and with illumination; or that it is "occidental"—which would connect it with the setting of the sun and shadow—for it is the

Essence itself. Now, as to the Essence, one cannot assign any particular status to it since it cannot be grasped by the intellect, and assigning status to that which is unintelligible is impossible. It is neither of the orient nor of the occident, neither necessary nor contingent, neither being nor non-being. It does not manifest itself by something without also manifesting itself by its contrary.

Nearly—that which was close to being produced but was not. "The oil": that which feeds the "lamp" mentioned above. *Shines*—the Essence only manifests itself by itself and for itself, without being associated with anything whatsoever—I mean by this an association in a purely conceptual mode. *Without even being touched by the fire*—this is an allusion to the manifested forms with which that which is symbolized by the oil is associated, the oil representing the essential reality of the lamp. The light of the lamp does not appear unless it is in contact with the fire. In its turn, the fire does not illuminate and does not manifest itself without the presence of something which feeds it, and this thing itself does not manifest itself unless the fire is in contact with it. *Light upon light*—the light attributed to the heavens and to the earth is identical to the absolute Light which is not limited by either the heavens or the earth. *Upon* (*ʿalā*): means "We" (*bi-maʿnā naḥnu*).[132]

Allāh guides by His instructions and His theophanies *whom He wills* from among his servants *towards His Light*—His absolute light and not the relative light attributed to some particular thing. *Allāh makes symbols for men*—so that the reality of things might be evident to them, for "Allāh knows all things," and knows how to make symbols for them. But to men He said, "Do not make symbols for Allāh." (Kor. 16:74) He formulated this interdiction because of their ignorance, for they would not know how to make these symbols; but this interdiction only applies to the Name Allāh, which is the totalizing Name. As for the other Names, there is no interdiction.[133]

Allāh is most Knowing and most Wise!

Mawqif 103.

26

The Theophanies and their Receptacles

And your Lord creates whatsoever He wills and chooses.

(Kor. 28:68)

Know that the act and absolute choice belong to God, so long as He does not Himself limit Himself by manifesting in a theophanic place or does not determine Himself by a particular determination. In that case, He is no longer a free Agent, but can only act according to the measure of the essential predispositions (*isti*ʿ*dādāt*)[134] and according to the nature of the receptacles of His theophanies. This conditioning by the essences[135] of the things imposes itself on God Himself and it is in conformity with what they are that He manifests Himself in them. In everything His act and His choice are according to what the essence of that thing demands. In fact, the universal predispositions are not extrinsic to the things. His acts are determined by His knowledge[136] and His knowledge, in its turn, is determined by its object. Surely, He can bring forth a fruit from a stone—but not before having changed the stone into a tree. Therefore, know the essential realities and feel their subtleties!

Mawqif 227.

27

The Minaret of the Divine Names

The alms are only for the poor . . .

(Kor. 9:60)

Know that whoever asks for something which is necessary to him because he cannot exist, subsist or manifest without it—whether this demand is formulated or not—is "poor" with respect to that thing. If the one who gives it to him is God, we say the He is the Benefactor and the Generous. If it is a creature who gives, we say of that creature that he gives alms (*fa-huwa mutaṣaddiq*), a word which is etymologically related to *ṣidq* "force", for a man does not give alms and does not give to another without doing violence to himself. In fact, as God has said: "The souls are prone to greed" (Kor. 4:128); "Those who have guarded their souls from greed, they will prosper" (Kor. 59:9) [. . .].

Allāh has granted a gift to the substance by giving existence to the accident without which the substance could not exist, in the same way that he has granted a gift to the accident by giving existence to the substance without which the accident could not subsist. He has granted a gift to the divine Names in existentiating the universe, for they can only manifest themselves through it and can only act in it.

Those who give alms are divided into several groups. One group gives alms out of mercy for those to whom they give alms but also with the hope of the recompense promised by Allāh. They do not distinguish, in giving alms, between the believer and the infidel, between him who obeys the Law and him who breaks it, since they believe that the order has been given to man to freely choose the beneficiary of the alms.[137]

A second group, of a more elevated rank than the first, includes those who give alms in order that the individual form of the beneficiary should subsist and continue to glorify Allāh and invoke Him. They do not distinguish in this respect between the believer and the infidel, between the animal endowed with reason and that which has none—better yet, between the animals and the vegetables. For they believe that each form, whatever it may be, glorifies Allāh as long as it subsists.[138]

Finally, there is a group that is even more elevated than all the others—and rare are those who belong to it! It is made up of those who give to the beneficiary of their alms in order that the manifestation of the divine Names should endure. The divine Names can, in fact, only manifest through the created forms, and if the "minaret" of a particular Name is destroyed, its effects disappear.[139]

Mawqif 312.

IV

On God and the Gods

28

He is that . . .

Your God is one God; there is no god but He.

(Kor. 2:163)

Say: It has only been revealed unto me that your God is one God.

(Kor. 21:108)

Say: I am only a man like you; it is revealed to me that your God is one God.

(Kor. 18:110)

Proclaim that there is no God but Me.

(Kor. 16:2)

In these verses and in other analogous verses, God addresses all those who have been reached by the Koranic revelation or earlier revelations—Jews, Christians, Mazdeans, idolaters, Manicheans and other groups professing varied opinions and beliefs with respect to Him—to teach them that their God is one in spite of the divergences of their doctrines and creeds concerning Him. For His essence is unique, and the divisions in relation to Him do not involve divisions of His essential reality. All the beliefs which are professed about Him are for Him just different names. Now, the multiplicity of names does not imply multiplicity of the

Named! He has a Name in all languages, which are infinite in number, but that does not affect His unicity.

The preceding verses allude to that which is taught by the elite—that is, the Sufis—namely the Unicity of Being (*waḥdat al-wujūd*) and the fact that He is the essence of everything "worshipped" and that, consequently, whatever he may take as the object of his worship, every worshipper worships only Him, as is proved by the following verse: "And your Lord has decreed that you will worship only Him." (Kor. 17:23)[140]

Since God decreed that every worshipper worships only Him, it is impossible that any other than Him be worshipped since the occurrence of anything which would be contrary to His decree is excluded. Those who are destined for perdition are such, therefore, solely by reason of their disobedience to the commands and prohibitions which have been brought by the Messengers of Allāh, since no one is an infidel in every respect.[141]

He is—may He be exalted!—the essential reality of everything whose existence is conceivable, imaginable or perceived by the senses, the One who does not multiply Himself or divide Himself. He is at the same time all things that are contrary and all things that are alike; and there is nothing other than that in the universe. He is at the same time "the First and the Last, the Apparent and the Hidden" (Kor. 57:3); and there is nothing other than that in the universe.[142] The places where He manifests Himself do not limit Him, the opinions and the beliefs of the ancients or the moderns do not contain Him. Thus, as He teaches us in an authentic *ḥadīth*,[143] He conforms to the opinion which each believer has of Him and with what the tongue of each speaker says of Him, for the opinion and the speech are His creations. Every representation which is made of Him is really Him, and His presence in this representation does not cease if the one who represented Him in this way later represents Him otherwise: He will be equally present in this new representation. He is limited for someone who believes and represents Him to be limited, absolute for someone who believes Him Absolute. He is substance or accident, transcendent or immanent, He is pure concept; or He resides in the heavens, or on the earth, and so on, in conformity with each of the innumerable beliefs and doctrines.

This is why someone has said, "Each time that something comes to your mind regarding Allāh—know that He is different from that!" This saying is rich in meaning in the order of essential truths. If it was spoken by a gnostic, he was worthy of speaking this way. If this was not the case, this is because it sometimes happens that God lets certain truths be spoken by people who are not worthy, in order to make these truths known to those who are worthy. The theologians who affirm the absolute transcendence of God through the speculative way—and not through conformity with the sacred Law—discuss this saying among themselves thinking that it is a proof in favor of their notion of the absolute transcendence of God. However, it does not mean at all what they imagine. Its true meaning is that God is not contained in any one particular belief or doctrine but that He is, in a certain respect, whatever someone says who speaks of Him or whatever each believer believes. Whatever comes to your mind regarding Allāh, His essence and His attributes, know that He is that and that He is other than that! He who maintained the saying that we have reported did not wish to say that Allāh is not that which comes to your mind, but that He is that and at the same time He is other than that for someone whose opinion differs from yours. Allāh is not limited by what comes to your mind—that is to say, your creed—or enclosed in the doctrine you profess. For the author of this saying, Allāh is other than that which comes to your mind [not for you, but] for him who professes a belief different from yours: both are in fact equally valid. "Difference" here is understood to mean everything which is mutually incompatible, whether it is the incompatibility of contraries, of opposites, of divergent terms or that of things that are alike—for, according to the logicians, things that are alike also are mutually incompatible.

In conclusion: If what you think and believe is the same as what the people of the Sunna[144] say, know that He is that—and other than that! If you think and believe that He is what all the schools of Islam profess and believe—He is that, and He is other than that! If you think that He is what the diverse communities believe—Muslims, Christians, Jews, Mazdeans, polytheists and others—He is that and He is other than that! And if you think and believe what is professed by the Knowers *par excellence*—prophets, saints and angels—He is that! He is other than that! None of His creatures worships Him in all His aspects; none is unfaithful to Him in all His aspects. No one knows Him in all His aspects; no one is ignorant of Him in all His aspects.

Those who are among the most knowing regarding Him have said: "Glory to Thee. We have no knowledge except what You have taught us." (Kor. 2:32)[145]

Each of His creatures worships Him and knows Him in a certain respect and is ignorant of Him in another respect. He created the creatures only that they should know Him and worship Him. Therefore, everyone necessarily knows Him in a certain respect and worships Him in this same respect. Because of that, error does not exist in this world except in a relative manner. But, in spite of that, anyone who strays from what has been brought by the Messengers will certainly go to perdition, and anyone who is in accordance with it will certainly be saved. "And Allāh embraces all and He is all-knowing." (Kor. 2:115,247, etc.) He embraces the beliefs of all His creatures, just as His mercy embraces them all. "He embraces everything by His mercy and His knowledge." (Kor. 40:7) He is the Glorious, and none of His creatures can know Him as He knows Himself, nor can they worship Him as would be fitting to His grandeur and His majesty. He is the Subtle, who manifests Himself by the very thing by which He hides Himself, and who hides Himself by the very thing by which He manifests Himself. There is no God but Him! O perplexity of perplexities! He Himself does not embrace His own essence.[146] How then could the weakness of creatures embrace Him?

Mawqif 254.

29

The God Conditioned by Belief

> *Say: we believe in that which has been revealed to us and in that which has been revealed to you: your God and our God are one God, and we surrender* (muslimūn) *to Him.*
>
> (Kor. 29:46)

What we are going to say comes from subtle allusion (*ishāra*) and not from exegesis (*tafsīr*) properly speaking.[147]

God commands Muhammadans to say to all the communities who belong to the "People of the Book"—Christians, Jews, Sabeans and others, "We believe in that which was revealed to us"—that is in that which epiphanizes itself to us, namely the God exempt from all limitation, transcendent in His very immanence, and, even more, transcendent in His very transcendence, who, in all that, still remains immanent; "and in that which was revealed to you"—that is, in that which epiphanizes itself to you in conditioned, immanent and limited forms. It is He whom His theophanies manifest to you as to us. The diverse terms which express the "descent" or the "coming" of the revelation[148] do not designate anything other than the manifestations (*ẓuhūrāt*) or the theophanies (*tajalliyāt*) of the Essence, of His work or of one or another of His attributes. Allāh is not "above" anything, which would imply that it is necessary to "climb" towards Him. The divine Essence, His word and His attributes are not localizable in one particular direction from which they would "descend" towards us.

The "descent" and other terms of this type have no meaning except in relation to the one who receives the theophany and to his spiritual rank. It is this rank which justifies the expression "descent" or other analogous expressions. For the rank of the creature is low and inferior while that of God is elevated and sublime. If it were not for that, there would be no question of descending or "making [the Revelation] descend," and one would not speak of "climbing" or "ascending"; "lowering" or "approaching."

It is the passive form [in which the real subject of the action expressed by the verb remains hidden] that is used in this verse, since the theophany in question here is produced starting from the degree which integrates all the divine Names.[149] Originating from this degree, the only Names which epiphanize themselves are the name of the divinity (the name Allāh), the name *al-Rabb* (the Lord) and the name *al-Raḥmān* (the All-Merciful). [Among the scriptural evidence for the preceding] Allāh has said: "And your Lord will come," (Kor. 89:22) and, similarly, one finds in a prophetic tradition: "Our Lord descends..."[150] Allāh has further said, "Only if Allāh comes," (Kor. 2:210) etc. It is impossible for one of the divine degrees to epiphanize itself with the totality of the Names which it encloses. He perpetually manifests certain of them and hides others. Understand!

Our God and the God of all communities contrary to ours are in truth and reality one unique God, in conformity to what He has said in numerous verses, "Your God is one unique God" (Kor. 2:163; 16:22; etc.). He also said, "There is no God but Allāh" (*wa mā min ilāhin illa Llāhu,* Kor. 3:62). This is so in spite of the diversity of His theophanies, their absolute or limited character, their transcendence or immanence and the variety of His manifestations. He has manifested Himself to Muhammadans beyond all form while at the same time manifesting Himself in every form, without that involving incarnation, union or mixture. To the Christians He has manifested Himself in the person of Christ and the monks, as He said in the Book.[151] To the Jews, He has manifested Himself in the form of ᶜUzayr [Ezra] and the Rabbis. To the Mazdeans He has manifested Himself in the form of fire, and to the dualists in the form of light and darkness. And He has manifested Himself to each person who worships some particular thing—rock, tree or animal—in the form of that thing, for no one who worships a finite thing worships it for the thing itself. What he worships is the epiphany in that form of the attributes of the true God—May He be exalted!—this epiphany representing, for each form, the divine aspect which properly corresponds to it. But [beyond this diversity of theophanic forms], He whom all of these worshippers worship is One, and their fault consists only in the fact that they restrict themselves in a limiting way [by adhering exclusively to one particular theophany].

Our God, as well as the God of the Christians, the Jews, the Sabeans and all the diverging sects, is One, just as He has taught us. But He has manifested Himself to us through a different theophany than that by which He manifested Himself in His revelation to the Christians, to the Jews and to the other sects. Even beyond that, He manifested Himself to the Muhammadan community itself by multiple and diverse theophanies, which explains why this community in its turn contains as many as seventy-three different sects.[152] Indeed, within each of these it would be necessary to distinguish still other sects, themselves varying and divergent, as anyone who is familiar with theology can confirm. Now, all of that results only from the diversity of theophanies, which is a function of the multiplicity of those to whom they are destined and to the diversity of their essential predispositions. In spite of this diversity, He who epiphanizes Himself is One, without changing, from the eternity without beginning to the eternity without end. But He reveals Himself to every being endowed with intelligence according to the measure of his intelligence. "And Allāh embraces all things, and He is All-Knowing." (Kor. 2:115)

Thus the religions are in fact unanimous regarding the object of worship—this worship being co-natural to all creatures, even if few of them are conscious of it—at least insofar as it is unconditioned, but not when it is considered in relation to the diversity of its determinations. But we, as Muslims, as He has prescribed, are subject to the universal God and believe in Him. Those who are destined for punishment are so destined only because they worship Him in a particular sensible form to the exclusion of any other. The only ones who will understand the significance of what we have said are the elite of the Muhammadan community, to the exclusion of the other communities.[153] There is not a single being in the world—be he one of those who are called "naturalists," "materialists" or otherwise—who is truly an atheist. If his words make you think to the contrary, it is your way of interpreting them which is flawed. Infidelity (*kufr*) does not exist in the universe, except in a relative way. If you are capable of understanding, you will see that there is a subtle point here, which is that someone who does not know God with this veritable knowledge in reality worships only a lord conditioned by the beliefs which he holds concerning him, a lord who can only reveal himself to him in the form of his belief. But the veritable Worshipped is beyond all of the "lords"!

All this is part of the secrets which it is proper to conceal from those who are not of our way. Beware! He who divulges this must be counted among the tempters of the servants of God. No fault can be imputed to the doctors of the law if they accuse him of being an infidel or a heretic whose repentance cannot be accepted. "And God says the Truth, and it is He who leads on the straight way." (Kor. 33:4)

Mawqif 246.

30

Concerning "Learned Ignorance"

> *And they have not measured Allāh to his just measure.*
>
> (Kor. 6:91)

This verse means: They have not proclaimed the Grandeur of God in a way which befits Him, according to what His essence demands and what is due to His majesty. In any case, this is impossible for them. It is not in the power of a contingent being to arrive at this. His essential predisposition (*isti*ʿ*dād*) does not permit it.

The third person plural of the pronoun in "And they have not measured" includes all the angels, the Spirits lost in love[154] and, below them, the jinn and men, including the Messengers, the prophets and the saints. Further, it embraces even the first Intellect, the Spirit of holiness, who is the first of the created beings and the nearest of the Near.

In fact, he who proclaims grandeur does so in the measure of the knowledge he has of that whose grandeur he proclaims. Now, any created being—whether he is among those whose knowledge is the fruit of reason or among those whose knowledge comes from theophanies—does not truly know Allāh. That is, he does not know Him as He knows Himself. How could a finite being know Him who is exempt from all relation or limitation? Did not the wisest of the creatures with regard to Allāh (i.e. the Prophet) say, "Glory to You! We do not know You as it would be fitting to know You. No praise embraces You. You are such that You are Your own praise, and that which is in You is beyond my reach."[155]

All the species of the universe glorify Him, and each affirms His transcendence in relation to what others profess about Him. What one affirms is precisely what is denied by another. This comes from the fact that everyone is veiled, regardless of the degree to which he has attained. He who professes pure transcendence is veiled, he who professes pure immanence is veiled, and he who professes both at the same time is also veiled. He who professes that He is absolute is veiled, and so is he who attributes limitations to Him, and so is he who denies one and the other. Whoever puts Him under some statute is veiled, in a measure which is determined by his rank and his place in relation to God. For there are as many different veils as there are those who are veiled. And let one not object that what I have just been saying is also a way of putting Him under a statute, for I will respond that what I have said does not proceed from me. It is He Himself who affirms this when He says, "And their knowledge does not embrace Him" (Kor. 20:110); "And Allāh puts you on guard against Himself," (Kor. 3:28)[156] which dispenses us from searching to attain that which is inaccessible. His Messengers have told us the same thing. When it is a question of the Essence of Allāh, the entire universe is stupid. There is nothing, up to the supreme Pleroma (*al-malāʾ al-aᶜlā*),[157] which is not in search of Him. Now, one only searches for something which is absent from the place where one is searching!

This search has no end: the knowledge of God has no end. He can not be known. He can only be known by that which proceeds from Him, as effects of His names, not His ipseity. This is why the following order was given even to the Prophet, although he possessed the knowledge of the First and the Last: "Say, 'Lord, increase me in knowledge!'" (Kor. 20:114) And he does not stop saying this, in every state, every station, every degree; in this world, in the intermediate world and in the beyond.

This being the case, what is required of us is to attach ourselves firmly to the way of faith, to accomplish the prescribed works and to follow the example of him who brought us the Law. That which he said we also say, to conform ourselves to his example and as simple interpreters of his word—for it is he who said it, and not us. And what he has kept in silence, we keep in silence—all the while applying the sacred legislation and the legal penalties, and awaiting death.

Mawqif 359.

V

On Secondary Causes

31

Divine Knowledge and Divine Decree

> *The associators will say: If Allāh had willed, we would have associated nothing with Him, nor would our fathers; and we would have prohibited nothing [of that which He had declared permissible].*
>
> (Kor. 6:148)

This speech [which God places in the mouth of the polytheists] is a case of a truthful statement formulated with the intention to lie. It means, in fact, "If Allāh willed that we should not be associators then we would not be; and if He willed that we should not prohibit what is permitted, we would not do it." And that is true. The untruthful aspect of this truthful statement is that they consider that everything which God wills for His servants satisfies Him and is pleasing to Him. And this is false. God wills for His servants that which His knowledge teaches Him concerning them from all eternity. And what His knowledge teaches Him concerning them from all eternity is what is demanded by their essential realities and what is determined by their predispositions—whether it be good or evil, belief or unbelief. His will conforms to His knowledge, which in turn conforms to its objects.[158] Sometimes the objects of His knowledge are on the straight way. And sometimes they are from among those who have strayed; sometimes they profess the divine Unity and sometimes they are polytheists; some are destined for punishment, others for happiness, some are truthful and others are liars. For the creatures are the places where His Names manifest themselves and, among these Names, some imply Beauty and Mercy—which is the lot of the elect, the "People of the right Hand"[159]; while other Names imply Majesty and Force—which is the lot of the damned, the "People of the left Hand." The fact that He wills a thing is not the sign that He loves that thing or that it pleases Him. He is not pleased by infidelity on the part of His servants and nevertheless His will is that many of them should be infidels. His will is simply the sign that from all eternity He knew with a prior knowledge that which He wills and what He would will eternally and forever. If everything which He willed from His servants were good, it would follow that the sending of the Messengers and the promulgation of the sacred Laws would be in vain. However, these Laws did come, bringing prescriptions and prohibition and discriminating between the "right Hand" and the "left Hand." Did He not say, "Some among them are destined for misery and some for happiness"? (Kor. 11:106)

That which Allāh—May He be exalted!—has told us [in the verse which opens this chapter] concerning the polytheists[160] and their opinions, according to which all that Allāh wills for His servants is good, represents one of the three positions on this problem. The position of the people of the Sunna is that He wills good as well as evil for His servants. The position of the Mu'tazilites is that He only wills good for them, and that evil proceeds from their wills and not from that of God.[161]

If Allāh—May He be exalted!—unveiled to one of His servants of the elite that which His knowledge knew in advance concerning him—that is to say, that which the "immutable prototype" (*ʿaynuhu al-thābita*) of that being demands—then it would be just and pleasing to God if this servant said, "I have done what I have done through the will of God and by His order"[162]; an order which transcends the categories of the good and the blamable. But to the polytheists He said: "Do you have knowledge? Well then, show it to Us!" (Kor. 6:148) This means: do you have knowledge concerning that which your essential predispositions imply?

Have your "immutable prototypes" been unveiled to you? Have you given associates to God, prohibited that which you have prohibited, done what you have done, only after God unveiled to you His will concerning you—this will being itself subordinated to [that which He knew of you in] His Knowledge? The secret of the divine Decree, which is the cause of causes, derives from this knowledge. Since that which the polytheists professed was not of this nature, and they acted as they did only on the basis of a simple opinion, Allāh said to them, "You have simply followed an opinion." (Kor. 6:148) This means: you have committed the sin of associationism and prohibited that which you have prohibited only on the basis of an opinion. Now, opinion is the most lying form of discourse, for it proceeds from psychic suggestions which the devil inspires in his friends.[163] The case of these polytheists being as Allāh has told us it is, they cannot justify themselves by invoking as proof the fact that Allāh willed that they should be polytheists and that He willed that they should lie concerning Him when they unduly prohibited that which they prohibited. On the contrary, it is Allāh who has a proof against them, and this is why He said: "Say, 'the decisive proof belongs to Allāh.' " (Kor. 6:149) By implication, to Allāh belongs the decisive proof against you, concerning your polytheism and all your disobediences to His orders and His interdictions. For He only willed for you that which your immutable prototypes demand through the "tongue of their states."[164] Allāh, being the Generous *par excellence*, does not reject the demand of the essential predispositions. In other words, He does not reject demands of the Names and the particular divine aspects which constitute the principial realities from which the creatures receive their realities. Thus He has only judged them in relation to themselves. Or, to say it better: you are your own judges. And the judge is constrained to judge each case according to what is imposed by the nature of that case.

Mawqif 236.

32

Concerning the Attribution of Acts

It is Allāh who has created you, you and that which you do.

(Kor. 37:96)

This and other similar verses have been perplexing to both the intellect and the imagination. Opinions regarding these verses are varied and their interpretations diverse. This is because Allāh attributes to Himself the creation of His servants and their acts while, at the same time, He affirms that their acts belong to them [since He uses the second person pronoun—that which *you* do—and thus assigns to his servants the acts whose creation He nonetheless claims]. Thus He affirms that something is without division at the same time that He declares that it is divided. The reason for this is that He sometimes acts without an intermediary and sometimes acts with an intermediary. In the latter case, He remains veiled behind the creatures through which He acts. Some have concluded from this that the act belongs properly to the creature behind whom He veils Himself, even if the creature is only the form in which the act is perceived in a sensible mode. On the other hand, others consider the act to be common to both God and the created form in whom He manifests Himself.

Now, the act (*al-fiᶜl,* a word which, in the technical lexicon of the grammarians, also designates the verb) in truth belongs to God alone. The universe is nothing other than the acts of Allāh [or "the verbs" of Allāh] and they are all intransitive. Their only reality is in Him, just as the intransitive verbs, which are sufficient in themselves, have no need of complements. Allāh has no transitive acts [or "verbs"], which would imply a complement distinct from Him and of which one could say that it is "other." The subject and the object are logically distinct. For example, the cabinet maker has as his complementary object the chest which he makes and which is necessarily distinct from him. But Allāh has no "other" nor does he have a "complement" endowed with a separate existence. This is why the masters of contemplation contemplate God manifesting Himself as Agent, Maker and Creator in all the atoms of the universe, without in any way casting doubt on the sanctity and the transcendence which belong to Him by right. [If such a contemplation is possible, it is because] every agent manifests itself by its act. Now, the act of Allāh has no reality other than in Him alone [without necessitating an "object" which would be the complement of the divine Subject] and it is inseparable from Him.

Allāh is the Apparent by His act for those whom He wills from among His servants. And He is the Hidden who veils Himself by His act for those whom He wills from among His servants, so that they imagine that the world is "other than Him" and "aside from Him"; but this is not so. In truth, the universe is like the infinitive of the grammarians, which is by definition a pure concept devoid of real existence. Similarly, the universe, which is the creative and formative act of Allāh, is only a concept devoid of all autonomous reality and has no existence except in and through the Subject who accomplishes it, that is, God. It is not "other than Him" or "aside from Him." It is as in the acts of standing or sitting, which [being pure accident] have by definition no existence of their own. It simply happens that the subject who at one time appears without this accidental characteristic later appears with it.

In the Koran and in the sayings of the Prophet, the acts are sometimes attributed to God through the intermediary of the creature and sometimes to the creatures through the intermediary of God. There has also been much confused clamor and considerable divergence over which is the correct attribution. He who knows what is meant by the word "creature" and what it truly is knows the truth of this matter. But this knowledge only belongs to the group of those whom Allāh filled with His mercy. May he grant that we may be counted among them!

It was said to me in a vision, between waking and sleeping (*wāqiᶜa*), "If Allāh has sometimes attributed the acts to His creatures, it is only because they are the forms and the aspects of the unique Reality."

Mawqif 275.

33

On Evil

It is reported in the Ṣaḥīḥ[165] *that the Prophet—On him be Grace and Peace!—said: "If one of you becomes aware of an evil, let him oppose it by force (literally: 'by his hand'); and if he cannot do that, let him oppose it by speech; and if he cannot do that, let him oppose it by his heart—this is the least which faith demands."*[166]

It is incumbent upon the sultan and the holders of authority, who have been established precisely for this purpose, that they oppose evil by force. The opposition of evil by speech belongs to the doctors of the Law whose knowledge is recognized and who manifest it in public. Lastly, to oppose evil by the heart is proper to ordinary believers once they are able to recognize what is evil and this opposition by the heart consists in reproving in their interior hearths those acts or those words which the religion prohibits. For the ordinary believer that is part of his faith in the Muhammadan revelation.

This obligation is not incumbent upon one who does not belong to any of these three groups, namely, one who [in every act] contemplates the unique true Agent. Opposition to evil by force on the part of the holders of authority, or by speech on the part of the doctors, brings profit for the community and for the one who commits the evil. Opposition to evil by the heart only brings profit to the ordinary believer himself, in that it reinforces his faith by the conviction that evil is prohibited and thus forestalls every inclination to evil on his part. But the fact of not opposing evil in one's heart does not in itself result in the ruin of any of the pillars of the Sacred Law nor does it have the effect of making licit what is illicit.

The Imām of the gnostics, the shaikh Muḥyī l-Dīn, said, when speaking of the secret of numbers: "When a man combats his own passion, he should give pre-eminence to the even number"—which means that he should give precedence to the simultaneous contemplation of the Lord and the servant over the "odd," which is the contemplation of the Lord alone—"and when he combats the passion of others, the authority of the odd should prevail over that of the even"—which means that he should give precedence to the contemplation of the Lord alone, thus bearing witness to the divine Unicity.[167] One of the gnostics also said: "He who looks at sinners with the eye of the Law, hates them; he who looks at sinners with the eye of essential Truth, excuses them."

He who arrives at the true knowledge of the divine Unicity and knows the meaning of the sayings: "Allāh has created you, you and that which you do" (Kor. 37:96); "They do not have power over anything that they have acquired" (Kor. 2:264); "It is not you who have killed them, but it is Allāh who has killed them" (Kor. 8:17); "You do not will unless Allāh wills" (Kor. 76:30); " Is it not to Him that the creation and the commandment belong?" (Kor. 7:54); "Say: all things proceed from Allāh" (Kor. 4:77), as well as other verses which indicate that God alone acts. He who knows this with a knowledge based on spiritual experience (*dhawq*) and on direct vision (*shuhūd*), and not upon imagination and conjecture, knows that the creatures are nothing other than the receptacles of the acts, the words and the intentions which God creates in them and over which they have no power even though, on the other hand, God calls them, imposes obligations on them, or gives them orders.

In these conditions, there is no place for man to defend jealously either the rights of God or his own rights; unless he is one of those who is invested with power and authority, or one of the exoteric learned men who make themselves known publicly as such, or if he is one of the ordinary believers. In these cases, he will try to oppose himself to evil by conformity and submission to the orders of the Legislator, by virtue of the profit which he has been told he will find in that. But if he does not belong to one of these three groups, opposing himself to evil amounts to associating with God something other than Him and to denying the divine Unicity. In fact, the divine Unicity excludes the opposition to evil by the heart, since it excludes the attribution of the act to its [apparent] agent. There is no being which could "oppose itself," since the one single Reality is the unique Agent of all the acts which are attributed to creatures. If there were an agent other than God, there would no longer be the divine Unicity. That which provokes the opposition to evil by the heart is the existence of the act, but there is no Agent [for this act] if it is not God.

This question is one of those which the initiates consider the most difficult.[168] But the gnostic who possesses the sense of spiritual discrimination knows how to distinguish the places and the circumstances and what each of them imposes as an obligation. To each place, and to each moment, he renders what is due.

Mawqif 133.

34

On Secondary Causes

And when they entered [into the city] in the manner which their father had prescribed, this precaution did not render them in any way independent of Allāh; it only satisfied a need which Jacob felt in his soul, for he possessed a knowledge which We had taught him—but most men know not!

(Kor. 12:68)[169]

The entrance [of the sons of Jacob into the city] "in the manner which their father had prescribed to them" signifies their entrance by different gates. It "did not render them in any way independent of Allāh"; that is to say, that this precaution could not negate the effect of the pre-eternal decree concerning them. Jacob—on him be Peace!—was not ignorant of this but desired to instruct his children in the sense of proper spiritual conduct and to make them progress to the summit of perfection. Now, this is just as incompatible with the recourse to secondary causes and exclusive confidence in them as it is with their abandonment pure and simple. To depend totally on secondary causes amounts to denying the divine Omnipotence—and one of the Names of Allāh is the "All-Powerful" (*al-qādir*); and to abandon them entirely amounts to denying the divine Wisdom—He is also called "the Wise" (*al-ḥakīm*). If He has chosen to establish the secondary causes and to veil His omnipotence behind them, it is not in vain.

Jacob's way of acting differs from the habitual practices of the masters of the Way. These masters prescribe that at first the disciple should renounce secondary causes completely in order that he establish himself firmly in the station of absolute Trust in God (*tawakkul*). Then, when he is firmly established there, the master has him return to recourse to secondary causes with respect to exterior comportment, while his heart remains with the Cause of the causes.[170] This method is necessary because of the weakness of the disciple and his distance from the light of Prophethood. This is not the case with the sons of Jacob, since they are [by virtue of their lineage] a part of Prophethood and what is difficult for others is not difficult for them. This is why Jacob prescribed for them that they should at the same time have recourse to a secondary cause and have absolute trust in God alone, which is the most perfect attitude. Thus he told them to "enter by different gates"—this precaution constituting a recourse to a secondary cause—while at the same time ordering them to place their trust only in God and to rely on Him to the exclusion of the secondary cause: "The decision belongs only to Allāh, in Him alone I put my trust, and let those who trust put their trust in Him alone!" (Kor. 12:67)

Such was the inner need which Jacob satisfied. The Knowers through Allāh—and *a fortiori* the prophets—are in fact the most merciful of beings with respect to other creatures and especially to their close relatives, who are most worthy of being well treated. Thus God ordered his Messenger Muḥammad—On him be Grace and Peace!—to begin his mission by first addressing himself to his family: "And warn your nearest kin." (Kor. 26:214) The Prophet then went up on the mountain of Ṣafā and successively called to Islam his daughter, then his paternal uncle, then the Banū ᶜabd Manāf, then the tribes of Quraysh.

In this verse, after having recounted the history of Jacob and his sons, Allāh praised the knowledge of Jacob—and there is no higher praise, for knowledge is the most elevated of the degrees—thus refuting what is imagined by weak minds for whom the exterior practice of trust in God is worth more than its inner practice while at the same time continuing to have recourse to secondary causes externally. This fallacy prevails among most men: "But most men know not!"

Then Allāh accorded to Jacob a supplementary honor by pointing out that his knowledge did not proceed from reason and reflection and that he had not received it from another creature, but that God Himself had instructed him. "But most men know not" that Allāh Himself takes charge of the teaching of certain of His servants, and that the knowledge that He teaches is the only true knowledge, for it is the immutable Knowledge which no doubt can shake and no uncertainty can touch.

Mawqif 269.

35

The Return to God

> *If, when they had been unjust toward themselves, they had come to you and asked pardon of Allāh, and the Messenger had asked pardon for them, they would have found that Allāh welcomes their repentance* (tawwāban) *and is All-Merciful* (raḥīman).
>
> (Kor. 4:64)[171]

"If when they had been unjust toward themselves": in committing acts which the divine Law prohibits, or in not performing the acts prescribed by God, "they came to you"; if they came to your way (*ṭarīqatika*) and the traditional rules which you have established (*sunanika*), and whether you [Muḥammad] are living or dead, firmly resolved to renounce their prior disobediences, repenting, running to take you as a guide and to follow you—in words, in acts, and in their spiritual states (*aḥwāl*)—the veil which covers their interior vision (*baṣāʾirihim*) would be lifted.[172] They would see things as they are, they would know the essential realities as they are.

If, once this unveiling has taken place, "they asked pardon of Allāh" (*fa-staghfirū Llāha*), then they would "hide themselves" in Allāh, that is to say that Allāh would become their "hiding place," for to pardon means [etymologically] "to hide" (*wa-l-ghafr al-satr*).[173]

From that point on, the acts which are attributed to them would be attributed to Allāh in conformity with what proceeds in reality: they would know that everything which proceeded from themselves was demanded by their essential predispositions, which are nothing other than the forms through which the divine Names manifest themselves. Now, these Names, in their turn, are nothing other than the forms of the supreme Essence. Thus it is in this very Essence that they will find where to hide themselves. They will reenter into the Essence in the same way that the shadow reenters into that which projects it,[174] since each act, and that which makes the act necessary, will then return to the Essence. The decree (*qaḍā*) and the decision (*ḥukm*) are in fact in conformity with that which this Essence demands for Itself and with that which It decides.

"And if the Messenger had asked pardon for them"—if, living or dead, the Messenger had asked for them that they should be "hidden," that is to say that they should arrive at that sublime spiritual degree by means of his aid and his direction—[175] "they would have found that Allāh welcomes their repentance (*tawwāban*)" [which signifies etymologically] that He is "returning"[176] from anger to contentment, from vengeance to mercy. For He abrogates what He wills by what He wills, He effaces what He wills and confirms what He wills. That which, from the point of view of His Law, would be called disobedience, will then be called "obedience" from the point of view of His will and of His commandment. He transforms the bad actions into good actions: "For them, Allāh will transform their bad actions to good actions." (Kor. 25:70)

The cause of this transformation is the fact [for the beings in question] of having arrived at the degree we have described. He who attains this degree will not know misfortune.

This transformation only affects the form and the legal status [of the acts considered]. A major fault will therefore be changed into a major good action and a minor fault into a minor good action.[177] According to tradition, the man who has achieved this spiritual station will say [on the day of the Last Judgment]: "O my Lord! I have committed faults. How is it that I do not see them here?"

"That is a grace of Allāh. He grants it to whomsoever He will. And to Allāh belongs an immense grace!" (Kor. 57:21)

Mawqif 168.

VI

On the Prophet

36

On the Imitation of the Prophet

> *Verily, you have in the Messenger of Allāh an excellent model.*
>
> (Kor. 33:21)[177bis]

I have received this precious verse through a secret spiritual modality. In fact, when Allāh wishes to communicate an order or an interdiction to me, announce good news or warn me, teach me some knowledge or respond to a question that I have asked Him, it is His practice to remove me from myself—without my exterior form being affected—and then to project on me that which He wishes through a subtle allusion contained in a verse of the Koran. After that, He restores me to myself, furnished with this verse, consoled and filled. He then sends me an inspiration concerning that which He wished to tell me through this verse. The communication of this verse proceeds without sound or letter and cannot be assigned to any direction of space.[178]

I have received in this manner—and it is due to the Grace of Allāh—about half of the Koran, and I hope not to die before I possess the entire Koran in this way. I am, through the favor of Allāh, protected in my inspirations, assured of their origins and of their ends, and Satan has no hold on me, for no demon can bring the word of Allāh. For no demon can transmit the revelation; for them that is totally impossible.

With rare exceptions, I have received all of the verses of which I speak here [i.e., in this work] through this modality. The People of our Way—may Allāh be pleased with them!—have never claimed to bring anything new in spiritual matters, but simply to discover new meanings in the immemorial Tradition. The legitimacy of this attitude is confirmed by the saying of the Prophet according to which the intelligence of a man is not perfect until he discovers multiple meanings in the Koran, or by that other *ḥadīth* reported by Ibn Ḥibbān in his *Ṣaḥīḥ*,[179] according to which the Koran has "an exterior and an interior" [literally: a back, *ẓahr*, and a front (stomach), *baṭn*]; a limit and a point of ascension. It is further confirmed by this saying of Ibn ᶜAbbās:[180] "No bird flutters its wings in the sky without our being able to find it inscribed in the Book of Allāh." It is confirmed also by this request (*dūᶜa*) that the Prophet addressed to Allāh in favor of Ibn 'Abbās: "Make him perspicacious in matters of religion and teach him the science of interpretation (*taᶜwīl*)." Similarly, in the *Ṣaḥīḥ*, it is mentioned that ᶜAlī[181] was asked: "Did the Messenger of Allāh grant you privileges, you People of the House (*ahl al-bayt*), by a particular knowledge which had not been granted to others?" He responded: "No—by Him who cleaves the seed and creates every living being!—unless you wish to speak of a particular penetration into the meanings of the Book of Allāh."

Everything which is found on this page, and everything which is found in these *Mawāqif*, is of this nature. It is Allāh who speaks the Truth, and it is He who guides on the straight path.

As for one who wishes to verify the veracity of the People of the Way, let him follow them! The People of the Way do not reduce the literal meaning [of the sacred Book] to nothing. Nor do they say: "The meaning of this verse is what we have understood it to mean, to the exclusion of all other meaning." Quite to the contrary, they affirm the validity of the exoteric sense that conforms to the literal meaning of the text and limit themselves to saying: "We have perceived a meaning in addition to the literal sense." It is evident that the Word of Allāh is in the same measure as His knowledge. Now, His knowledge embraces equally the necessary things, the possible things and the impossible things. We can even go so far as to maintain, consequently, that in a given verse Allāh wished to say everything that both the exotericists and the esotericists have understood by it—and in addition, everything which has escaped both of them. This is why each time a being comes along in whom Allāh has opened the interior vision (*baṣīra*) and illuminated the heart, one sees him draw from a verse or a *ḥadīth* a meaning which no one before him had been led to discover. And it will be thus until the rising of the Hour! Now, all this is due to the infinite character of the knowledge of Allāh, who is their Master and their Guide.

[Returning to the introductory verse of this chapter] we will say that it has, in spite of its brevity, the character of an inimitable miracle (*iʿjāz*) which cannot be comprehended,either in a direct manner or through symbolic allusion. It is an immense ocean, without beginning or end. Everything which can be written about the sciences of this world and the other is contained in this incomparable allusion.

"Verily, you have in the Messenger of Allāh an excellent model." This relates, in the first place, to the manner in which God treats His Messenger. Sometimes He fills him, sometimes He deprives him; sometimes He tests him and sometimes He helps him. Sometimes He confronts him with his enemies and the combat sometimes concludes with his victory and sometimes with his defeat. Sometimes He contracts him, and sometimes He expands him.[182] Sometimes He grants what he asks and sometimes He refuses it.

Sometimes He says to him, "Verily, those who make a pact with you, in truth it is with Allāh that they make the pact"; "Whoever obeys the Messenger, he indeed obeys Allāh" (Kor. 4:80); "Say: if you love Allāh, follow me and Allāh will love you" (Kor. 3:31); "It is not you who threw, when you threw, but it is Allāh who threw." (Kor. 8:17) The force of the expression shows that this means: "You are not you when you are you, but you are Allāh!"[183]

And sometimes He says to him: "Verily, you do not guide those whom you love [but it is Allāh who guides whom He wishes]" (Kor. 28:16); "You have no part in this matter: either He will pardon them or He will punish them" (Kor. 3:128); "You cannot make the dead hear, nor make the deaf hear when they have turned their backs" (Kor. 27:80); "And it is not you who can lead the blind out of their error" (Kor. 27:81; 30:53); "Is it you who will save those who are in the fire?" (Kor. 30:19); "And it is not you who is all-powerful over them!" (Kor. 50:45)

Thus God sometimes places the Messenger at His own sublime level, and sometimes at the level of a lowly servant. From this point of view the introductory verse embraces infinite and inaccessible knowledge; comprising knowledge of Allāh, His attributes, His independence with respect to His creatures and their dependence on Him; and knowledge of the Messengers, what is incumbent on them, what is permitted to them and what is prohibited to them; and knowledge of the divine Wisdom in the creation, and the procession of this world and of the other world.

"Verily, you have in the Messenger of Allāh an excellent model." From another point of view this model concerns the comportment of the Messenger towards his Lord, the perfect Realization of what servitude means,the accomplishment of everything which Lordship demands, his total dependence upon God (*al-faqr ilahyi*) and his total abandonment to Him in all things, his submission to His power and his satisfaction in everything He decrees, his gratitude for the graces which He grants and his patience in the trials which He inflicts. This aspect of the verse relates to the limitless and innumerable sciences concerning the sacred Law and concerning acts of worship and the ordinary acts of existence, practices leading to salvation and practices leading to perdition.

"Verily, you have in the Messenger of Allāh an excellent model." From yet another point of view, this relates to the comportment of men toward the Prophet. Some proclaimed that he was truthful, and others accused him of lying. Some loved him while others hated him, causing him to suffer by their words and their acts and causing him to experience all the torments, with the exception of death. They struck him in his noble face, and broke his teeth. Coalitions were formed against him. People close to him abandoned him. But all of that only resulted in making his vision of his task more clear and his spiritual state more firm. This category of interpretation of this verse is connected to the inexhaustible knowledge of the virtues of the Prophet and of his teachings and the virtues and teachings of the other prophets and gnostics, and of the trials which they all had to endure from those who treated them as impostors.

"Verily, you have in the Messenger of Allāh an excellent model." This can also be understood as the comportment of the Prophet toward the creatures, of the love which he had for them, of the good that he wished for them—to such an extent that his Lord said to him: "Perhaps you are consumed with grief because they do not believe" (Kor. 26:3)—and of his patience toward them. He saw in them the face of God.[184] Men treated him unjustly and he was forgiving. They refused him and he was generous to them. They did not recognize him and he endured their ignorance, they excluded him and he brought them together. He said: "O my God, pardon my people, for they do not know what they do." He answered evil with good and offenses with kindness, clothing himself with the divine attributes (*takhalluqan bi-l-akhlāq al-ilahiyya*) and realizing the divine Names of Mercy (*taḥaquqqan bi-l-asmāʾal-raḥmāniyya*)—for no one is more patient than God in the face of insult. This aspect of the verse is connected to the knowledge—which pens cannot transcribe nor minds enclose—of the noble attributes and perfect virtues, and to the science of the governing of men in the affairs of religion as well as the affairs of the world with a view toward good order and the prosperity of the universe and the happiness of the elect.

For the disciple—indeed, for the gnostic himself—this verse should be the cardinal point of his orientation (*qiblatahu*) in every place, the object of his contemplation at every instant. All of the spiritual states which he can know are connected in fact to one of the four aspects of which we have spoken. This verse can represent the straight way along which Satan waits in ambush to assail from four sides the sons of Adam, for he has made this oath: "Assuredly, I will wait in ambush for them along Your straight path, then I will assail them from the front, from behind, from their right and from their left. And You will find that most of them are not grateful toward You." (Kor. 7:16–17)

He who conforms to that which this verse indicates belongs to the number of the grateful (*al-shākirīn*); and for him, the demons have no power over him.[185]

Mawqif 1.

37

Concerning Extinction in the Prophet

I am going to teach you the interpretation of that which you were unable to endure with patience.

(Kor. 18:79)

In my youth I loved to study the works of the spiritual masters—may Allāh be pleased with them!—even before I followed their way. In the course of this study I happened to come across sayings emanating from the greatest of them that made my hair stand on end and oppressed my soul, in spite of my faith in their words according to the meaning which they wished to give to them; for I was convinced of their perfect sense of right spiritual conduct and of their eminent virtues. This was the case, for example, in this phrase of ᶜAbd al-Qādir al-Jīlī:[186] "O you Prophets! The exalted title has been conferred on you, but we have been given something that was not given to you!" Or further, there is the saying of Abū l-Ghayth b. Jamīl:[187] "We have plunged into an ocean upon whose shores the prophets have halted!"[188] Or indeed in this saying of Shiblī speaking to his disciple: "Do you attest that I am Muḥammad Messenger of Allāh?" To which the disciple responded, "I attest that you are Muḥammad Messenger of Allāh."[189]

Everything written by those who attempt to interpret such sayings did not suffice to appease my soul. It went on like this until the moment when God granted me the grace of sojourning at Medina—may it be blessed![190] One day, when I was in retreat (*khalwa*), turned toward the *qibla*, invoking Allāh, He ravished me from the world and from myself. Then He returned me to myself and immediately I said, in the declarative mode and not in the narrative mode, "If Mūsā b. ᶜImrān (Moses) were alive, he could not do otherwise than follow me."[191] I knew then that this saying was part of what subsisted in me of the ecstatic rapture that I had just experienced. I was "extinguished" in the Messenger of Allāh and, at that moment, I was not a certain person; I was Muḥammad—On him be Grace and Peace! If this had not been so, I could only have spoken these words in the narrative mode, that is to say, by reporting them as having come from the Prophet.

The same thing happened another day with another saying of the Prophet: "I am the head of the sons of Adam, and I say this without boasting." In this way the manner in which one should interpret the sayings of the masters became apparent to me. I mean by this that my own case served me as a model and example, and not that I compare my spiritual state to theirs.[192] Far from that! Far from that! Far from that! Their station is higher and more glorious, their state more complete and more perfect!

This is the explanation ᶜAbd al-Karīm al-Jīlī[193] enunciates when he writes, "When two beings encounter each other in one of the perfect spiritual stations, each becomes identical to the other in that station. He who understands what that means understands the sense of the saying of Ḥallāj and others."[194]

Before the saying that I have reported sprang forth from me, when I was turned toward the Noble Garden[195] during the third night of the month of Ramaḍān, a spiritual state accompanied by tears came upon me. Allāh projected into my heart a saying which the Prophet addressed to me, saying, "Rejoice in a victory!"[196] Two nights later, I invoked Allāh when I was asleep. I had a vision in which the noble person of the Prophet merged with mine to the point that we became a single being. I looked at myself and I saw him having become me. Taken with fear and with joy at the same time, I got up, made an ablution and entered the mosque to salute the Prophet—may Grace and Peace be upon him! I returned to my retreat and began to invoke Allāh.

God tore me from myself and the world, then returned me to myself after having projected upon me His saying, "Now you have brought the Truth." (Kor. 2:71) I knew that this projection was a confirmation of my vision.

The next day, God ravished me from myself in the customary way and I heard a voice which said, "Look at what I have hidden in order that you may be that" (*unẓur mā aknantuhu ḥattā kuntahu*) employing literally this blessed and assonant form. I knew that this saying confirmed the preceding vision—May God be praised!

Now God ordered me to proclaim the graces which I had received from Him by virtue of the general sanction which He gave to the Prophet: "And as for the grace of your Lord, proclaim it!" (Kor. 93:11) In fact, every order which He addresses to the Prophet is an order for his community excepting only those which clearly concern him exclusively. But, in addition, God gave this order to me in particular on several occasions by means of this noble verse: "And as for the grace of your Lord, proclaim it!"[197]

Mawqif 13.

38

Concerning Abandonment to God

> Muslim reported, following Rāfi^c b. Khudayj: "*The Prophet—On him be Grace and Peace!—arrived in Medina at the time when the people were fertilizing the palm trees. He said to them: 'What are you doing?' They answered: 'We are fertilizing the palm trees.' He said to them: 'Perhaps it would be better if you didn't do that!' Therefore, they stopped doing it, and the harvest of dates diminished. The Prophet—On him be Grace and Peace!—then said to them: 'I am only a man. When I order you to do something that is related to your religion, follow that order. But when I order you to do something that proceeds from my personal opinion, know that I am only a man!'* "[198]

In another recension, also reported by Muslim, there is the following variation: "I am only a man like you, whose opinion can be correct or in error. I did not say to you, 'Allāh said . . . ' for I do not lie with respect to Allāh."[199]

If someone concludes from these two *ḥadīth*s that the Prophet was ignorant of the fact that fertilization is usually profitable for palm trees according to the way that Allāh has arranged things in His wisdom and His generosity, that person is far from the truth. However, if the one who speaks this way is one of the spiritual men, he undoubtedly means something else. For how could the Messengers be so ignorant of the affairs of this lower world? Muḥammad grew up in Arabia, which is the land of palm trees, in the area where they best know how to cultivate them and fertilize them. Such a conclusion regarding him is therefore absurd. In addition—as I was inspired to know yesterday in a vision between waking and sleep—the knowledge of the Prophet is partly drawn from the sciences of the Qalam (the Pen) and of the Tablet,[200] which include precisely the knowledge of the affairs of this lower world, of their causes and of their effects. But the Prophet—On him be Grace and Peace!—knew to what an extent the Arabs relied on secondary causes. The Muslims had only recently come out of paganism and worship of idols. Therefore, he wished to teach them that secondary causes by themselves are not efficacious and that God is the only Agent, whether secondary causes are present or not. Thus he said to them: "Perhaps it would be better if you didn't do that!" thinking that if they abandoned their reliance on a secondary cause—in this case the fertilization—God would accomplish a miracle,[201] and that the palm trees would be improved without the intervention of fertilization. After this he would redirect the Muslims to the practice of secondary causes. In this way they would attain the station of abandonment to God (*tawakkul*). This state consists in relying exclusively on God, whether in the presence or the absence of secondary causes. In other words, this state consists in relying externally on secondary causes while at the same time relying inwardly on God. It does not consist in refraining from action on the grounds of having confidence in God.

This is why the Prophet did not categorically order the Muslims to abandon all reliance on secondary causes. It would be inconceivable, in fact, that he should totally prohibit reliance on them since they have their place in the economy of the divine Wisdom and since we find nothing which is without a cause. The secondary causes are demanded by the divine Wisdom and it is God who instituted them. To deny them would be pure ignorance, and this ignorance in relation to God is inconceivable for the Prophet.

If he said "I am only a man . . . " in the first *ḥadīth* and "I am only man like you . . . " in the second, it is because they did not understand what he wished from them and, on the other hand, they imagined that everything which the Prophet said was a revelation (*waḥy*) from Allāh and a teaching coming from Him. He therefore explained that he was man and Prophet. Everything in his words which relate to the commandments and the prohibitions, to the institution of the Law, to divine pronouncements, all of that is part of the revelation which he had received the order to transmit. Everything which related to spiritual discipline, to the government of souls, and to the ascent toward the stations of perfection, came from himself—On him be Grace and Peace! In this way he taught them that they should not consider what he said as always belonging to the Revelation, or as always proceeding from himself.

He was sent to all men without exception, Whites or Blacks. He speaks to each according to his predisposition and instructs each according to his capacity, governing each in the way that would be profitable to him. He addresses himself to the great and the humble, to the king and his subjects, to the learned and the ignorant, to the intelligent and the fool. He speaks pleasantly with children, with the old and with women. In relation to everything which he orders or prohibits by divine order or teaches as coming from Allāh, he is Prophet. In everything which relates to the government of his community, to its education, to its organization, he is man and what he says comes from himself—but by virtue of a general mandate which God has granted him.

The Sufi masters are inspired by this example in their way of teaching their disciples. They begin by having them renounce secondary causes, for they consider that one who enters the way is not able truly to attain—to the point where it would become permanent—the station of abandonment to God, while at the same time giving himself to secondary causes. Then, when the disciples are stronger, their masters authorize them once again to have recourse to secondary causes while at the same time inwardly relying on God alone, which corresponds to the station of the perfect among the prophets and saints. The recourse to secondary causes joined to exclusive confidence in God is unanimously recommended by the masters and even judged obligatory by certain of them.

This story is different from the story of Jacob—On him be Grace and Peace!—when he said to his sons: "Do not enter by one gate only . . . " (Kor. 12:67) for Jacob taught them at once to utilize secondary causes while at the same time having exclusive confidence in God. The reason he was able to do it that way was the force of their interior light and their participation in prophethood without intermediary.[202]

Mawqif 278.

39

Unitive Vision and Separative Vision

> *The Ṣaḥīḥ of Muslim reports this saying of the Prophet—On him be Grace and Peace!:* "Moments of oppression overcome my heart. Then I ask pardon of Allāh and return towards Him, repenting, more than one hundred times a day."[203] *Other recensions of this tradition exist.*

Know that the word *ghayn* [the root of the Arabic verb used at the beginning of this *ḥadīth*] designates a "covering", a "clothing"—whether this "covering" be of the order of sensible things or of the order of spiritual realities as is the case here. It happens, in fact, that at certain moments, the Prophet is crushed by the vision of the immensity of the divine Lordship (*rubūbiyya*) and by what is implied by the absolute servitude (*ʿubūda*) which the divinity of Allāh demands, taking into account the diversity of the effects produced by His names. For it is necessary to do justice to all these effects and to all of the theophanic places, in spite of their contradictory character. Seeing all that, the Prophet then considered the weakness and the powerlessness of the servant to acquit himself of even a part of the infinity of duties towards his Lord and God at the same time that he must endure his adversaries, keep company with his supporters, respect the divine order to unite them and to attract their hearts in spite of their natural aversions, the difference of their intentions and the divergence of their goals; and all that while looking out for his family and for himself!

What the Prophet sees in this contemplation is so immense that a man, as such,[204] cannot endure it in any way. He then asks "pardon" of Allāh, which means [if one interprets it conforming to the etymology of the verb *istaghfara* which is used here] that he asks of Allāh—that is, of the Name which encloses all the divine Names—to "veil" him in order that this trying and exhausting contemplation in distinctive mode (which the Name of Allāh implies) should cease. In fact, this Name is that of the degree of the "function of divinity," and this function demands an object (*maʾlūh*) upon which to exercise itself.[205] For every "worshipped" demands a "worshipper." These two terms are inseparable and correlative.

Allāh, after having veiled him with respect to this contemplation of the "function of divinity," then grants him the unitive and blessed contemplation of the Essence and introduces him into the presence of the totalizing divine ipseity in which the Names and their effects are annihilated and the stars, the suns and the moons are swallowed up;[206] where the Messenger, the message, and the receiver of the message are but one. For in the "He" (*huwa*) of the Essence,[207] there are no more distinctions and this is why the Prophet said: "I return towards *Him,*" employing the pronoun "Him." This means: I return there where there is no longer Worshipped or worshipper, neither Lord nor servant. The disappearance of the worshipper brings about the disappearance of the Worshipped,[208] just as in grammar the disappearance of the first term of a genitive construction brings about the disappearance of the second.

But, in conformity to His wisdom it was right that afterwards the Prophet should be sent back from the vision of pure Unity and that he should return—this is the meaning of his "repentance" [*tawba,* which also means "return"]—toward the separative vision.[209] For, He created men and jinn only that they should worship Him and know Him—and, if they remained at the degree of pure Unity, there would be none to worship Him. In this separative vision, the Worshipped and the worshipper, the Lord and the servant, the Creator and the creature are again perceived. It is the vision at this degree which permits the operation of these distinctions, for it is the degrees that differentiate and separate [the unique Reality].

In this way the Prophet acquits himself of his duty to Lordship, satisfies the demands of the "function of Divinity" and does justice, as far as human capacity can, to what is demanded by the ontological degrees, the theophanic places and the effects of the divine Names.

The Prophet—On him be Grace and Peace!—went continually from one of these visions to the other, which is expressed by the number of times each day mentioned in the recensions of this *ḥadīth*. Such was his state at the beginning of his apostleship. Ibn Qanīᶜ reported that the Prophet said: "My Lord sent me with a mission (*risāla*) and it weighed me down."

It is because of the crushing character of the separative vision, and all that it implies concerning duties towards God and towards the creatures, that certain of the Prophets and the saints went so far as to desire never to have existed; for they had lost sight of the fact that existence is a good, a mercy and a blessing, and that non-being is an evil and a punishment.

I have already commented on this same *ḥadīth* in another section of this book, providing an interpretation which is in contradiction with this one.[210] That was under the effect of an inspiration contradictory to the one which comes to me now. I do not write according to my desire but as I am inspired:

> Sometimes I am Yemenite, if I meet a man from Yemen, and sometimes I am ᶜAdnānite, if it is a son of Maᶜadd that I meet.[211]

It is not astonishing that the Prophet, who knew both of these states [corresponding to the unitive vision and the separative vision], should have spoken of them both in a single speech which is the synthesis of their meanings: he had received the "Sum of Speech" (*jawāmiᶜ al-kalim*),[212] and all the fountains of Wisdom were given to him, whereas every person, excepting him, knows only "the particular place where he must drink" (Kor. 2:260 and 7:160) and takes the path which is reserved for him.

It could be that this *ḥadīth* secretly contains still other meanings. May Allāh inspire them to those whom He chooses from among His servants!

Mawqif 253.

VII

I Am God, I Am Creature . . .

40

I am God, I am Creature . . .

I am God,[213] I am creature; I am Lord, I am servant

I am the Throne and the mat one treads on; I am hell and I am the blissful eternity

I am water, I am fire; I am air and the earth

I am the "how much" and the "how"; I am the presence and the absence.

I am the essence and the attributes; I am the near and the far

All being is my being; I am the Only, I am the Unique.[214]

Notes

Introduction

1. See infra for the commentary on this verse in text 19.

1bis. Cited by M. Habart in his introduction to the French translation of the *Life of ᶜAbd al-Kadir* by Charles-Henry Churchill, 2nd ed. (Algiers, 1974), 36. Despite its inaccuracies, this work is of interest since it was written by a man who met the Amir for the first time in Bursa in 1853 and later had numerous interviews with him in Damascus in 1859–1860.

2. On the treaty of Tafna and the commission collected by Bugeaud, see Ch. A. Julien, *Histoire de l'Algérie contemporaine* (Paris, 1964), Vol. 1, 137ff.

3. Cited by Paul Azan, *L'Emir ᶜAbd el-Kader, du fanatisme musulman au patriotisme français* (Paris, 1925). In spite of an extremely biased point of view which is openly stated by the subtitle, this work is still useful due to the richness of the sources used (in particular official documents but also private correspondence and unpublished testimonies) which are listed on pages 286–295. On the other hand, the bibliography in the work of Ch. A. Julien, cited supra (pp. 532–534), contains a list of the principal publications in French which later contributed, sometimes on very important points (notably concerning the treaty of Tafna), to rectifying or clarifying the history of the Amir. Several books have appeared recently: *ᶜAbd al-Qadīr and the Algerians* by R. Danziger, New York and London, 1977, and two biographies published simultaneously (Paris, 1994), one by Bruno Etienne and the

other by S. Aouli, R. Redjala and Ph. Zoummeroff (each entitled *Abd el-Kader*). Most of these works, however, only concern the military and political activities of ʿAbd al-Kader. In what follows of this introduction we will refer to sources generally untapped until now, which will enable us, as they become accessible, to complete our knowledge of ʿAbd al-Kader.

4. Cited by M. Habart, ibid.

5. Léon Roche, *Dix Ans à travers l'Islam* (Paris, 1904), 191–192. While displaying the good conscience of a French patriot, Roche—whom France would make a plenipotentiary minister in Japan after a long Algerian career—allows some remorse to show through in his memoirs. Many years later this remorse would lead him to correspond with the Amir and to try—without success—to see him again.

6. Cf. Marcel Emerit, "La Légende de Léon Roche," *Revue africaine* (1st–2nd trimester, 1947), 81–105.

7. Léon Roche, *op. cit.*, 113–114.

8. Ibid., 140–141.

9. On the other hand, the French administration was very interested in the life of the Amir and constantly watched his activities through the French consulate or various agents. On this subject, see the texts cited by A. Temimi in the *Revue d'histoire maghrébine*, no. 15–16 (Tunis, 1979), 107–115: "L'emir ʿAbd el-Kader a Damas." M. Temimi published in the same review previously unpublished documents concerning ʿAbd al-Kader's life after he left Amboise: cf. *Revue d'histoire maghrébine*, no. 10–11: 157–202; no. 12: 308–343; and in no. 15–16, Arabic section: 5–33. Nonetheless, we regret the commentaries which he sees fit to attach to those letters in which the Amir expressed his need for money. The frugality and detachment of ʿAbd al-Kader no longer need to be proven—neither does the existence in Damascus of a large Algerian colony which, for the most part, lived on subsidies which the Amir freely provided.

9bis. Churchill, *Life of ʿAbd al-Kader*, 321.

10. Muḥammad b. al-Amir ʿAbd al-Qādir, *Tuḥfat al-Zāʾir fī taʾrīkh al-Jazāʾir wa l-Amīr ʿAbd al-Qādir* (2nd ed., Damascus, 1964), 596–597 (hereafter cited as *Tuḥfa*).

11. Some biographers, following Léon Roche, give the year of the Amir's birth as 1223/1808. We believe that the correct date is that of 23 Rajab, 1222 (1807), which is given by the son of ʿAbd al-Kader (*Tuḥfa*, 932).

12. *Tuḥfa,* 856, ff.; ᶜAbd al-Majīd b. Muḥammad al-Khānī, *Al-ḥadāʾiq al-wardiyya fī ḥaqāʾiq ajillāʾ al-naqshbandiyya* (Damascus, 1308 A.H.), 282. After the independence of Algeria the Amir's body was transferred to the cemetery of the *shuhadāʾ* in Algiers.

13. *Al-miqraḍ al-ḥādd* (Beirut, undated), 186.

14. Cf. *Tuḥfa,* 529 where the *ᶜAqīda sughra* of Sanūsī and the *Risāla* of Ibn Abī Zayd al-Qayrawānī are mentioned. In his letters, the Amir reiterates to his correspondents his desire to procure some books. Some books were provided to him by a Shaikh of Constantinople, Muḥammad al-Shādhilī, a fairly ambiguous personage about whom some information can be found in the study by Dr. Abū l-Qāsim Saᶜad Allāh (Algiers, 1974); his relationship with ᶜAbd al-Kader is discussed on pp. 51–60. Some specifics concerning the education of the Amir and his masters are found in the "Chevallier document" studied by Monsignor Teissier, the Bishop of Oran, in *Islamochristiana,* no. 1 (Rome, 1975), 41–69, under the title "L'entourage de l'emir ᶜAbd al-Qadir et le dialogue islamo-chretien." This document, presently kept at the National Library of Algiers, was communicated to us in 1965 by Jacques Chevallier who was then the mayor of Algiers. Since then, a facsimile edition was published by the Algerian authorities on the occassion of the centennial of the death of the Amir in 1983 with the title *Al-sīra al-dhātiyya li l-amīr ᶜAbd al-Qadīr.* However, the information which he provides concerning the Amir's masters is only related to the classical disciplines—*fiqh,* grammar, etc.—and not to the study of the works of *taṣawwuf.* The doctoral dissertation currently being prepared by an Algerian researcher, ᶜAbdelkader Benharrats, on Algerian society and the education of the Amir ᶜAbd al-Kader will undoubtedly provide precious information on the youth of the author of the *Mawāqif.*

15. We are alluding here to the thesis maintained by Dr. Abū l-Wafā Taftāzānī in an article ("Al ṭarīqa al-akbariyya," *Al-kitāb al-tadhkārī, Muḥyī l-dīn b. ᶜArabī* [Cairo, 1969], 295–353) which includes interesting documentary elements to which we will return, but which calls for a detailed critique, on the historical as well as on the doctrinal plane, which we cannot undertake in these pages.

16. The voyage in the course of which this meeting with the Said Murtada took place is mentioned in *Tuḥfa,* 929. For his help concerning the chain of transmission of the *khirqa akbariyya,* I must first express my thanks to Riyāḍ al-Māliḥ, of Damascus, who was kind enough to tell me of several contemporary *silsila*-s in

which the Amir plays a part. (These *silsila*-s will eventually be published in a work of Riyāḍ al-Māliḥ dedicated to Ibn ᶜArabī and entitled *Sulṭān al-ᶜĀrifīn*.) My gratitude also goes to my daughter, Claude Chodkiewicz-Addas, who undertook a meticulous and fastidious collection of the available sources on this subject. The principal documents which permit the reconstruction of this initiatic genealogy are the following:

1. On the chains of transmission of the *khirqa* that end with Ibn ᶜArabī: *Al-Futūḥāt al-Makkiyya* (hereafter cited as Fut.), 1: 185–187; *Al-durrat al-fākhira* (Section no. 69, 157 of the English translation by Dr. Austin published in London in 1971 with the title *Sufis of Andalusia*; this section appears on pp. 177 of the French version published in Paris in 1979 with the title *Les Soufis d'Andalousie*); *Kitāb nasab al-khirqa* (this unpublished work of Ibn ᶜArabī is also of interest because it presents the doctrinal views of the Shaikh al-Akbar on the idea of *khirqa* itself). These various sources indicate that Ibn ᶜArabī received the *khirqa*: (a) from Abū l-Ḥasan b. ᶜAbdallāh b. Jāmīᶜ who received it directly from Khaḍir; (b) from Taqī al-dīn al-Tawzarī with an *isnad* which also goes back to Khaḍir through two intermediaries; (c) also from Taqī al-dīn al-Tawzarī, with a "classical" *isnad* going back to the Prophet; (d) from Muḥammad b. Qāsim al-Tamīmī with an *isnad* which also goes back to the Prophet; (e) from Jamal al-dīn Yūnus b. Yaḥyiā al-ᶜAbbāsī, who received it from ᶜAbd al-Qādir al-Jilānī, prior to whom the *isnad*, as in the two previous cases, goes back to the Prophet.

2. On the chains of transmission starting with Ibn ᶜArabī and ending with the Amir (in addition to the documents communicated by Riyāḍ al-Māliḥ): Ṣafī al-dīn al-Qushshāshī (d. 1071/1660), *Al-simṭ al-majīd*, Hayderabad, 1367 A.H., 105; Murtaḍā al-Zabīdī (d. 1205/1791), *ᶜIqd al-jawhar al-thamīn* (s.v. *Hātimiyya Sadriyya*); Muḥammad b. ᶜAlī al-Sanūsī (d. 1276/1859), *Al-salsabīl al-muᶜīn fī l-tarāʾiq al-ᶜarbaᶜīn* in the margin of *Al-Masāʾil al-ᶜAshr*, Cairo, 1353 A.H., 70–72. The first link in these chains after Ibn ᶜArabī is, in all cases, his disciple Ṣadr al-dīn Qūnawi.

16bis. Even if we leave aside, due to its specific character, the *Wishaḥ al-katāʾib*, military regulations for the Amir's troops (French translation by V. Rosetty, *Le Spectateur militaire*, no. 2 [February 15, 1844]; reedited in Algiers, 1890), the works of ᶜAbd al-Kader, as they may be known to a French reader, do not foreshadow the

Mawāqif. The *Dhikrā l-ᶜāqil* (trans. by Gustave Dugat, Paris, 1858, with the title *Rappel à l'intelligent, avis à l'indifferent;* more recently translated by René Khawam, Paris, 1977, with the title *Lettre aux Français*) is, like the *Miqraḍ al-ḥādd* (not published in French) mentioned above, a work written for a specific situation. Apparently edited in Bursa, in response to an invitation by the Asiatic Society, this eulogy of knowledge—and particularly the knowledge of the *sharīᶜa,* the revealed Law—does not show any particular originality. Addressing himself, as in the *Miqraḍ,* to Europeans whose ability to understand the traditional teachings of Islam the Amir had good reason not to overestimate, he adopted a very didactic tone and method of exposition. The same remark applies to certain of his letters, in particular those which he addressed to the members of the Masonic Lodge of Henri IV (Arabic text published by A. Temimi, *Revue d'histoire maghrébine,* no. 15–16: 5–33, documents 9, 10, 11). Concerning the Amir's relationship with Masonry, it is useful to consult *L'Emir Abdelkader vu par le Grand Orient de France 1864–1865,* Bruno Etienne's presentation to the colloquium "French and American perceptions of the Maghreb-held in Princeton in April, 1982, as well as the work mentioned in Note 3.

17. *Al-ḥadāʾiq al-wardiyya*: 281. Concerning Shaikh Khālid (d. 1242/1827), in addition to the *ḥadāʾiq* (p. 224ff.), cf. A. Hourani, "Shaykh Khālid and the Naqshbandī Order," in *Islamic Philosophy and the Classical Tradition* (Oxford, 1972), 89–103; H. Algar, "The Naqshbandī Order: a Preliminary Survey," in *Studia Islamica* (Paris, 1976), 123–152; ᶜAbbās al-Ghazāwī, "Mawlawnā Khālid al-Naqshbandī," in *Majalla al-majmaᶜ al-ᶜilmī al-kurdī,* vol. 1 and 2 (Baghdad, 1974). The work (in Kurdish) of ᶜAbd al-Karīm al-Mudarris, *Yādī Mardān,* published in 1979 by the Kurdish Academy in Baghdad, includes writing in Arabic of Shaikh Khālid.

18. The most explicit chapter concerning this subject is *Mawqif* (hereafter abbreviated as M.) 18 (text 2 in this work).

19. *Fut.,* I, 248. This passage is part of the 44th Chapter (pp. 247–250), devoted to the *bahālīl,* in which Ibn ᶜArabī analyzes the three fundamental types into which the extreme diversity of individual cases can be reduced.

20. Extract of text 2. On the necessity of the spiritual master, see text 7.

21. The role which is played in the destiny of ᶜAbd al-Kader by the *ruḥāniyya* ("form" or spiritual "presence") of Ibn ᶜArabī,

who died six centuries earlier, arises from a type of realization well known in the *taṣawwuf*, that of the *uwaysiyya*. Among other similar cases, let us cite that of Bahā al-dīn Naqshband (d. 1389) who had several living masters but whose true Shaikh was the *ruḥāniyya* of a deceased master, ᶜAbd al-Khāliq Ghujdawānī (d. 1220).

21bis. About the Shaikh Muḥammad b. Masᶜūd al-Fāsī (who died in Mecca in 1289 A.H.), see Ḥassan b. al-Hājj Muḥammad al-Kūhan al-Fāsī, *Kitāb ṭabaqat al-Shādhiliyya* (Cairo, 1347), 197 ff.; and Yūsuf al-Nabhānī, *Jamiᶜ Karāmāt al-awliyāʾ* (Cairo, 1329 A.H.), I, 223. His own master, the Shaikh Muḥammad b. Ḥamza Ẓāfir al-Madanī, whose disciple he became in Tripoli in 1242, was himself the disciple of the Shaikh al-ᶜArabī al-Darqāwī (d. 1242 A.H.). Concerning the relations of these two personages see Martin Lings, *A Moslem Saint of the Twentieth Century* (London, 1951), 70–71 (pp. 85–87 of the French translation which appeared under the title *Un saint musulman du xx^e siecle* [Paris, 1973]). Concerning the relation of the Amir with the Shaikh Muḥammad al-Fāsī, see *Tuḥfat al-Zāʾir*, 695ff., where there is also the text of a *qaṣīda* composed by ᶜAbd al-Kader in honor of his master (reproduced with variations in the *Kitāb al-Mawāqif*, 1394ff. and in the *Dīwān al-Amīr ᶜAbd al-Qādir* [Damascus, undated], 135ff.).

22. The account of this voyage is given, with numerous digressions, in the *Tuḥfa*, 671–717, from which the following citations are extracted.

23. This improvised commentary will be the point of departure of M. 137, not translated here, but whose theme is identical to that of M. 132 (text 19).

24. Two sources furnish invaluable information about the process of composition of the *Mawāqif*. The first and the oldest is the already cited work by ᶜAbd al-Majīd al-Khānī—whose grandfather had known the Amir during his first journey to the east—and had even been charged by the Shaikh Khālid with the spiritual direction of the father of ᶜAbd al-Kader (ᶜAbd al-Majīd al-Khānī, op. cit, p. 281) and whose father, the Shaikh Muḥammad al-Khānī, is one of the three personages who requested permission of the Amir to write down his words. In addition, the Shaikh Muḥammad is the author of numerous questions, the response to which furnished material for some chapters of the *Mawāqif*. Finally, it was he who, after the death of ᶜAbd al-Kader, completed Volume 3 of the work by adding texts discovered in his

papers (cf. *Ḥadā'iq*, 282). Let us point out in addition that the passage of the *Ḥadā'iq* from which we have drawn this information is followed by the text of M. 365 (pp. 1288–1290 of the 2nd edition of the *Mawāqif*). The comparison of the two texts—the one given by the *Ḥadā'iq* is three times as long—confirms the suspicion prompted by the reading of several passages, that the printed editions of the *Mawāqif* had sections missing; not to mention editing and typographical errors.

The second of our sources is a recent book, that of Jawād al-Murābiṭ, *Al-taṣawwuf wa l-amīr ʿAbd al-Qādir* (Damascus, 1966), pp. 20–24, 89, but whose author made use of information coming from the grandfather of his uncle who was of Algerian origin and had followed the Amir to Damascus and was one of those close to him (p. 18).

25. This is clearly the case with the last chapter, M. 372, which undoubtedly is only a sketch. We have seen in the preceding note that there can exist versions of varying lengths of the same chapter. A critical edition would be necessary: neither the Egyptian edition of 1911 nor the edition of Damascus of 1966–67 deserve this name, in spite of the care which we are told went into them. Whimsical punctuation and innumerable blunders disfigure the text. In addition, variant readings are ignored, even though the way in which the work was constructed suggests that they would be numerous. The first edition was based on the manuscript of the Shaikh al-Bayṭār, annotated by the Amir (and financed by a sister of ʿIzzet Pāshā, the Governor of Damascus at the time when the Amir lived there). The second edition, if one believes the introductory notice, collated this text with one furnished by a manuscript which was copied by the Shaikh Muḥammad Saʿīd Jamal al-dīn al-Qāsimī. Although this detail was not specified, this copy, which is conserved at the Ẓahiriyya (no. 5323), and which is dated 1308 A.H., only corresponds to the first volume. Other more or less complete manuscripts, which we have not been able to consult, are also found in the Ẓahiriyya under the numbers 9236, 9264 to 9268, 1528–1530, 11424, 6995 (written during the life of the author).

Riyāḍ al-Māliḥ has informed us that he has examined a manuscript of the *Mawāqif* of a nephew of the Amir who is no longer living, the Amir Badr al-dīn al-Jazā'irī. But other private collections certainly contain manuscripts coming from those who were close to ʿAbd al-Kader. In addition, certain fragments of the *Mawāqif* have taken on an independent life under an autonomous title, such as *Sharḥ khutbat al-Futūḥat*, as was pointed out by Dr.

Osman Yahya at Ankara (*Histoire et Classification de l'oeuvre d'Ibn Arabī* [Damascus, 1964], I, 232) which is undoubtedly—but to what extent?—identical to Chapter 366.

Let us point out that C. Brocklemann, *Geschichte der Arabischen Litteratur,* Leyde, 1945–1949 (hereafter cited as G.A.L.), S II, 886 (the reference in the index to G.I., 502, is incorrect), does not mention the *Kitab al-Mawāqif* and that it is also ignored in the article of Encyclopédie de l'Islam (hereafter cited as E.I.), second edition, devoted to the Amir. Massignon is certainly the first Orientalist to mention the *Kitab al-Mawāqif* (cf. *Passion,* II, 350). He proposed, according to Vincent Monteil, to translate *mawāqif* as "reposoirs." This translation appears doubly inadequate to us. First of all, the word "reposoir" has the inconvenience of unduly christianizing the title of ᶜAbd al-Kader. But especially, the Arabic term designates, according to its etymology, a place where one stops in a standing position which is exemplified indeed by the rite of *wuqūf* at ᶜArafāt during the pilgrimage. This vertical immobility therefore, is not properly speaking a "repose," and to suggest such a meaning would furthermore contradict the Akbarian tradition of *mawqif* pointed out infra.

26. There is no doubt that the Amir himself chose this title. Allusions to "these *Mawāqif*" or to "another of these *Mawāqif*" abound in the text. Beyond that, Chapter 360 of the *kitāb al-Mawāqif* p. 1276 (second edition, Damascus, 1966–1967, in three volumes, hereafter cited as *Mawāqif*) gives some precise details: "It was said to me," writes the author (with him these words always introduce the recounting of a supernatural inspiration), "'Lengthen the title of your book [by calling it] *The Book of Stops, On Certain Subtle Allusions Concerning Secrets and Spiritual Knowledge Which are Concealed in the Koran.*' "

27. The first edition of the *Mawāqif* by Niffarī is that of Arberry (London, 1935). Nwyia published important unpublished fragments (in *Trois Oeuvre inédites de mystiques musulmans* [Beirut, 1973], 181–324). Concerning Niffarī's notion of *mawqif,* cf. Arberry, *op. cit.,* 14–15 of the introduction and pp. 9–16 of the Arabic text; Nwyia, *Exegese coranique et Language mystique* (Beirut, 1970), 359ff. Beyond the references to Niffarī which Ibn ᶜArabī himself made, the interest which the Akbarian school took in this author is remarkably illustrated by the commentary of ᶜAfīf al-dīn Tilimsānī on the *Mawāqif.* Extracts from this commentary were published also by Nwyia, *Bulletin d'études orientales,* vol. 30 (Damascus, 1978), under the title "Une cible d'Ibn Taymiyya:

le moniste al-Tilimsānī" ("A Target of Ibn Taymiyya: the Monist al-Tilimsānī").

28. *Fut.*, vol. 1, p. 392, vol. 2, 609.

29. *Mawāqif*, p. 1337.

30. Ibid., pp. 745, 826, 872, 946, 1158, etc.

31. Ibid., pp. 1155–1159.

32. Ibid., p. 1114.

33. Ibid., p. 1133.

34. Ibid., p. 1387.

35. Ibid., pp. 570, 946.

36. Ibid., p. 917. In order to understand the passage, it is necessary to remember that Ibn 'Arabī (*Fuṣūṣ al-ḥikam*, edited by A. A. ʿAfīfī, Beirut, 1946, hereafter cited as *Fus.*, vol 1, p. 47) declares that he had received this work from the very hand of the Prophet.

37. Ibid., p. 514. Is this *Book on the Rūḥ* the *Rūḥ al-rūḥ* mentioned by Ibn ʿArabī in his *Ijāza* which seems to be lost?

38. Ibid., p. 1133. Other cases of encounters in the subtle mode with the Shaikh al-Akbar are recounted pp. 1389–1390, probably following the notes collected by the Shaikh Muḥammad al-Khānī after the death of ʿAbd al-Kader.

39. We are thinking in particular of terms such as *tajallī, aʿyān thābita, fayḍ, istiʿdād,* which we will return to in the notes for the translation. (Concerning the technical vocabulary of Ibn ʿArabī, the thesis of Mme. Suʿād al-Hakīm, edited in Beirut in 1981 in a revised and augmented version with the title *Al-muʿjam al-sūfī: al-ḥikma fī ḥudūd al-kalima,* is informative.) We should also note the usage which ʿAbd al-Kader makes, in order to bring out the esoteric meaning of certain Koranic passages, of etymologies used for the same purpose by Ibn ʿArabī (for example, by the roots GhFR, JNN, KFR, etc.).

40. *Mawāqif*, pp. 1290–1336; cf. note 25.

41. Ibid., pp. 1337–1354.

42. Ibid., pp. 1194–1274.

43. Ibid., pp. 1161–1195.

44. Ibid., pp. 910–917.

45. Ibid., pp. 1152–1155.

46. Ibid., pp. 1017–1021.

47. Ibid., pp. 1021–1026.

48. Ibid., pp. 1195–1196.

49. Ibid., pp. 745–759, 826–841, 861–867, 870–875.

50. This work of Tirmidhī, which for a long time was thought to be lost and was only known through citations by Ibn ʿArabī, was rediscovered and edited by Dr. Osman Yahya (Beirut, 1965). Concerning Tirmidhī, who died at the beginning of the ninth century, the fundamental work is that of Bernd Radtke, *Ein islamischer Theosoph des 3/9 Jahrhunderts,* Freiburg, 1980. We are also indebted to B. Radtke for a new critical edition of the *Khatm al-awliyā,* included in *Drei Schriften des Theosoph von Tirmid,* Beirut, 1992. See also *Al-Ḥakīm al-Tirmidhī wa-naẓariyyatuhu fī l-Wilāya,* by Dr. ʿAbd al-Fattāh ʿAbdallāh Baraka, vol. 2 (Cairo, 1971), and *Al-maʿrifa ʿinda l-Ḥakīm al-Tirmidhī* of ʿAbd al-Muḥsin al-Ḥusayni (Cairo, undated). The responses of Ibn ʿArabī to the questions of Tirmidhī are found in *Fut.*, vol. 2, pp. 40–139.

51. On this manner of resolving the difficulties of certain Akbarian texts, cf. Shaʿrānī, *Al-Yawāqīt wa-l-jawāhir* (Cairo, 1369 A.H.), vol. 1, pp. 7, 61; vol. 2, pp. 182. Although the hypothesis of deliberate interpolations is used in a manner that is too systematic not to be suspect, and even though the examination of autograph manuscripts of Ibn ʿArabī in many cases allows this hypothesis to be categorically rejected, we have, nonetheless, several reasons to suppose that some interpolations were produced, voluntarily or not, due to the wide circulation of the writings of Ibn ʿArabī in the Shiite milieu. The work of critically editing the works of Ibn ʿArabī has barely begun and it is difficult for the time being to be more precise.

52. Cf. ʿAbd al-Majīd al-Khanī, Ḥadāʾiq p. 288 and Jawād al-Murābiṭ, Al-taṣawwuf p. 89 (gives as a date for this voyage the year 1288). The first of these sources allows us to determine that one of the two people in question was the Shaikh Muḥammad al-Ṭanṭāwī, who was born in Egypt in 1240, and attached to the *tariqa naqshbandiyya* in 1255 in Damascus (*Al-hadāʾiq al-Wardiyya,* 276), and who was, as we have said, one of the three men listening to the Amir to whom we owe the writing down of the talks given by ʿAbd al-Kader during his *majālis.* The Shaikh Ṭanṭāwī was to

play an important role in the Akbarian renewal which took place in Egypt at the end of the last century among those attached to the *khālīdīyya* branch of the *ṭarīqa naqshbandiyya* (we are referring to an article by Dr. Taftāzānī, cited in note 15, in which there is a detailed bibliography). The affirmation of ʿAbd al-Majīd al-Khānī is confirmed by the presence, in the first volume of a manuscript of the *Futūḥāt* kept in Damascus at the Ẓahiriyya (no. 142), of a letter sent by Muḥammad al-Ṭanṭāwī to ʿAbd al-Kader while he was at Qonya. This letter is dated the 19th of Ramaḍān, 1287.

53. *Mawāqif,* pp. 1112–1134.

54. Ibid., pp. 419–421. For Ibn ʿArabī the *Furqān,* that is, the Revelation in its discriminating aspect, drives away Iblīs (the devil) by virtue of its separating nature whereas the Koran, (*Qurʾān*) due to its unifying nature (which is implied by the meaning of the root QRʾ), calls him. This is the reason for the necessity of "taking refuge" (*istiʿādha*). Concerning the Koran as the unifier of the *haqāʾiq,* cf. *Fut.,* vol. 3, pp. 91–96. The difference which ʿAbd al-Kader establishes between *waḥdat al-shuhūd* and *waḥdat al-wujūd* corresponds to the difference which Ibn ʿArabī establishes between the "arrival" at God and the "return" to the creatures in Chapter 45 of the *Futūḥāt* (vol. 1, pp. 250–253).

55. It appears that it was used for the first time by Ṣadr al-dīn Qūnawī. In any case it is found in his *Miftāḥ al-ghayb* (see the thesis of S. Ruspoli, *La Clef du monde suprasensible,* Paris IV, 1978, p. 28 of the Arabic text, Sec. 42). One remark is required with respect to the translation of *waḥdat al-wujūd* as "unicity of being" and not, in accordance with common practice, by "unicity of existence." In the West, scholasticism only accepted towards the end the substitution of *existere* for *esse*—a substitution which unfortunately supposes an equivalence which classic Latin (in which *exsistere/existere* had the sense of "come from," "appear") did not admit. In every state of causation, *existere* and its French derivatives should, strictly speaking, only be applied to that which is "other than God." Thus it is entirely improper in the context of Akbarian metaphysics to render the *wujūd* of *waḥdat al-wujūd* as "existence," since *waḥdat al-wujūd* specifically precludes, as we will see in the texts translated here, that there is "some thing other than God." Furthermore, it is interesting to note that the fortune of "existence" in the philosophical vocabulary, starting from the seventeenth century, resulted from the concern with dissipating the confusion between "being" in the sense of *esse, actus essendi,* and "being" in

the sense of *ens* (itself a later Latin form), these two meanings corresponding respectively to those of *ειναι* and *τὸ ὄν* in Greek. Now, confronted with the problem of translating these Greek words, the Arab philosophers and theologians—after some hesitation which is very understandable given some particularities of the Arabic language—chose, at least after Fārābī (d. 950), to translate them as *wujūd* and *mawjūd*. (Both derived from the root WJD which has as its first meaning "find", "know." We will reserve the numerous commentaries which this evokes for a work dedicated to Ibn ᶜArabī.) On the historical facts of this question we refer to Charles H. Kahn, *On the Terminology for COPULA and EXISTENCE,* in *Islamic Philosophy and the Classical Tradition* (Oxford, 1972), pp. 141–158; F. Jabre, "Etre et esprit dans la pensee arabe" *Studia Islamica* 32 (Paris, 1970), pp. 169–180; E. Gilson, "Notes sur le vocabulaire du l'etre", *Medieval Studies* 8 (1946), pp. 150–158.

56. *Mawāqif,* pp. 129–130 (text 17 in this work).

57. Ibid., pp. 304–308. (For the commentary on the same verse by Ibn ᶜArabī, cf. *Fut.,* Chapter 558, the section devoted to the divine Name *ar-Raqīb.*) Another example of the very explicit formulation of *waḥdat al-wujūd* is in M. 238 (pp. 535–536).

58. Ibid., p. 131. We are referring here to the polemic unleashed in Cairo by the appearance of the first volumes of the critical edition of the *Futūḥāt.* See in particular the newspaper *al-Akhbār,* issues of 14 Nov. 1975, 8 March 1976, 9 April 1976 and 14 May 1976, and the series of five articles appearing in the first issues of 1976 of the review *Liwā ᵓal-Islām.* Concerning this controversy, see the article by Th. Emil Homerin, "Ibn ᶜArabī in the People's Assembly," *Middle East Journal,* vol. 40, no. 3, 1986, 462–477.

59. *Fut.,* I, p. 301.

60. For example, *Fut.,* vol. 2, pp. 410–411; *Fus.,* vol. 1, p. 201. One will find a very complete account of this problem in the article by D. Gril, "Le personnage coranique de Pharaon d'après l'interpretation d'Ibn Arabī", *Annales islamologiques,* vol. 14 (1978), pp. 37–57.

61. *Mawāqif,* p. 63. As regards Firᶜawn, see also a very curious passage of M. 265 (page 795). Concerning the polemic aroused by the position of Ibn ᶜArabī on the subject of the fate of Firᶜawn, one will find a characteristic sample of the opposing theses in Muḥammad ᶜAbd al-Laṭīf b. Al-Khatīb, *Imān Firᶜawn* (Cairo, 1963), which contains two treatises, one by Jalāl al-dīn al-Dawwānī favor-

able to Ibn ᶜArabī, and another which is hostile to Ibn ᶜArabī and was written in reply to the first by ᶜAli b. Sulṭān Muḥammad al-Qārī. Cf. also the *Kitāb al-Fatḥ al-mubīn,* (Cairo, 1304 A.H.), by the Shaikh ᶜUmar Ḥafīd al-Shihāb Aḥmad al-ᶜAṭṭār (p. 62).

62. See in particular *Fut.*, vol. 1, p. 656; vol. 2, p. 408; vol. 4, p. 248, and *Fus.*, p. 94.

63. *Mawāqif,* pp. 508–512; 937–977.

64. *Tarjumān al-ashwāq* (Beirut, 1961), p. 43.

65. *Fut.*, vol. 3, p. 132.

66. See for example *Fut.*, vol. 1, p. 415.

67. *Mawāqif,* p. 561, 767, 770, 1003, 1212. See texts 28 through 30 in this work.

68. Ibid., p. 768 (text 28 in this work).

69. *Al-hadāʾiq al-wardiyya,* 281.

70. Cf. the examples given for Egypt by Dr. Taftāzanī in the article mentioned in note 15.

71. This subject deserves a special study which we hope to make in the future. We limit ourselves here to drawing particular attention to two key personages: the Shaikh Muḥammad al-Ṭanṭāwī (cf. note 52) and the Shaikh ᶜAbd al-Raḥmān ᶜIllaysh (d. 1349 A.H.) who was present at the last moments of the Amir and who was at the origin of the interest which certain westerners began to have at the time in the work of Ibn ᶜArabī. ᶜAbd al-Kader already had some relation with the father of ᶜAbd al-Raḥmān al-ᶜIllaysh—the Shaikh Muḥammad ᶜIllaysh, the great Malikite Mufti of Egypt—at the time of his combats in Algeria. In fact, it was Shaikh Muḥammad ᶜIllaysh who, at the request of ᶜAbd al-Kader, issued the *fatwa* condemning the treason of the Sultan of Morocco (one can find in the *Tuḥfat al-Zāʾir,* p. 471, the text of the request for the *fatwa* and, p. 474, the *fatwa* itself. A well documented exposition of the relation between the Sultan and the Amir was given recently by R. Danziger under the title "Abd al-Qādir and Abd al-Raḥmān: religious and political aspects of their confrontation," *The Maghreb Review,* 1981, vol. 6, no. 1–2, p. 27–35). On the role of the Shaikh ᶜAbd al-Raḥmān ᶜIllaysh, important indications are found in the article by Michel Valsan, "L'Islam et la fonction de René Guénon," in *Etudes traditionelles* (Jan.–Feb. 1953), pp. 14–48. A part of the personal papers of the Shaikh

ᶜIllaysh were acquired through the intermediary of Dr. F. De Jong and are now found at Leyden where they are part of the collection Ms. Or. 14431. However, Dr. De Jong has told us that no document dealing with the relations between the Amir and the Shaikh ᶜIllaysh are found among these papers nor in the private Egyptian collection from which they came. On the other hand, a correspondence between the two men, which we have not yet been able to consult, appears in a private Syrian collection annexed to an unpublished manuscript of the Amir titled *Ḥusam al-dīn li-qatᶜ shaym al-murtaddīn.* (Although certain orientalists have retained the transcription *ᶜUllaysh,* the correct form is the one which we have indicated, conforming to information furnished by the father of Shaikh ᶜAbd al-Raḥmān in several of his works.)

72. The publication by Dr. William C. Chittick of the testament of Qūnawī ("The last will and testament of Ibn ᶜArabī's foremost disciple," in *Sophia Perennis* (Teheran, 1978), pp. 43–58) further confirms that Qūnawī formulated in an explicit manner the interdiction to designate for himself a *khalīfa* (see para. 2, p. 51 and note 30).

73. However, it is evident, as was underlined by Jacques Berque (*L'Intérieur du Maghreb,* Paris, 1978, Chapter XV; see particularly pp. 512–513) that the "literary splendor" of many passages of the *Mawāqif* "risks overturning the accepted hierarchies" and that the true *nahḍa* is undoubtedly not where it is sought. We take the opportunity provided by this remark to thank Professor Berque who, inviting us to give a lecture dedicated to the relationship between ᶜAbd al-Kader and Ibn ᶜArabī at the symposium organized by him at the College de France in 1977 on Amir ᶜAbd al-Kader in the East, gave us the opportunity to present a preliminary account of the research which is the basis of the present work.

74. Born in 1819, the shaikh Ahmad Gümüshkhanevī, who belonged to the *tariqa naqshbandiyya-khālidiyya,* was one of the most emminent spiritual masters in Ottoman Turkey in the nineteenth century. At his death in 1894, he was buried, by order of Sultan ᶜAbd al-Hamīd, whom he was close to, in the cemetery adjoining the Sulaymāniyya Mosque (his tomb is to the left of the entrance to the mausoleum of Salaymān the Magnificent). Concerning him, see the article by Irfan Gündüz in *Islam Ansiklopedisi,* Istanbul, 1986, and the article by Butros Abu-Manneh, *Shaikh Ahmad Ziya al-Din al-Gümüshkhanevī and the Khaladi Suborder* in Bulletin of

the *Israeli Academic Center in Cairo,* no. 6, 1985, p. 2–3. He is the author of a treatise on *taṣawwuf,* strongly influenced by Ibn ᶜArabī, the *Jamīᶜ al-usūl,* edited in Cairo in 1331 A.H., which also exists in an undated lithograph edition printed in Turkey. See on p. 49 of this latter edition, the passage on the *ṭarīqa akbariyya,* the word *ṭarīqa* to be taken here with the double meaning of *ṭarīq* ("way," defined as a metaphysical perspective and an initiatic discipline) and of *silsila* (expressing the regular transmission of the *baraka*) and not in the sense of "brotherhood." One of the many disciples of Gümüshkhānevī was the Shaikh Jūda Ibrāhīm (d. 1344 A.H.), known as *Shādhilī-naqshbandī-akbarī.* He was succeeded by his son ᶜIsā, who lives in Egypt in Minyā al-qamḥ. (An article is devoted to the Shaikh Jūda Ibrāhīm in Muḥammad al-Rakhāwi, *Al-anwār al-qudsiyya* [Cairo, 1344 A.H.], p. 263ff.)

75. *Mawāqif,* pp. 919. This citation of Ibn ᶜArabī is found in *Fut.,* vol. 3, p. 188.

Translation

1. The earth and the heavens symbolize respectively the "world of sensible manifestation" (*ᶜālam al-shahāda*) and the "world of occultation" (*ᶜālam al-ghayb*) to which correspond, microcosmically, the body and the spirit. Their "disappearance" is the consequence of their reabsorption in the Principle.

2. According to Ibn ᶜArabī (*Fut,* vol. 1, p. 169), who points out that this technical use of the words *ṭūl* and *ᶜarḍ* was instituted by Ḥallāj (concerning their meaning for him, cf. Massignon, *Passion,* index s.v., and more particularly vol. 3, p. 16, note 8): "the height (*ṭūl*) of the universe designates the spiritual world, that is to say the world of pure ideas and of the divine Commandment" and "the width (*ᶜarḍ*) of the universe designates the world of creation, of nature and of bodies." The annihilation of the two "dimensions" which order universal manifestation corresponds, in geometric symbolism, to their reintegration in the initial Point.

3. The supererogatory act (*al-nafl*) implies the autonomy of the one who accomplishes it. His "return" to the obligatory act (*farḍ*) which, in the Akbarian perspective, constitutes the matrix, implies the extinction of the creature and therefore the annihilation of all will of his own and the total identification with the divine Will. On this theme, see text 19.

4. The colors of the spectrum represent the apparent differentiation of white light. This new symbolic expression of the return to the Principle is reinforced by the connotations of the Arabic term *inṣibāgh*: these colors are "dyes" and therefore have an artificial character.

5. This expression is taken from a *ḥadīth qudsī,* that is to say, a saying of the Prophet in which God expresses Himself in the first person. Ibn ᶜArabī comments on this expression in the Fuṣūs (vol. 1, p. 112). For him it means the disappearance of our illusory relationship to ourselves and its replacement by the realization of our real relation to God.

6. The "saying of Ḥallāj" is evidently the famous *Anā l-Ḥaqq* which one can translate as "I am God" or "I am the absolutely Real." The context suggests that the saying which "was said" to the Amir is *Anta al-Ḥaqq,* "you are God" or "you are the absolutely Real." Concerning the saying of Ḥallāj, see text 16.

7. "The oft-repeated seven": this enigmatic expression has given rise to many interpretations, one of the most current being that it designates the *Fātiḥa,* the opening Sura of the Koran, which is comprised of seven verses (which, according to certain commentators were revealed *two* times; cf. Suyūtī, *Itqān,* chap. 11; Ibn ᶜArabī, *Fut.* vol. 2, p. 507, evokes the case of the Surats which were revealed two times but does not mention the *Fātiḥa*). Without being able to go deeply into this problem, let us point out especially the interpretation of Qāshānī (d. 1329) for whom "the repeated seven" are the seven attributes of the Essence (life, knowledge, power, will, hearing, sight and speech), while the "glorious Koran" mentioned later in the verse symbolizes the divine Essence itself (Qāshānī, *Tafsīr,* published under the name of Ibn ᶜArabī [Beirut, 1968], I, p. 670). The "repeated" is therefore an allusion to the reflection of the seven attributes in the person of the Perfect Man, who is the "mirror of God." But the Essence, which absolutely transcends all duality, does not repeat: in all metaphysical rigor, the "mirror of God" is not "other than God." Concerning the interpretations advanced by the orientalists, see E.I., second edition, s.v. *Kuran,* vol. 5, p. 403 and 426..

8. Ibn ᶜArabī (*Fut.,* vol. 2, 310–311) identifies the absolute Imagination as the "cloud" (*al-ᶜamā*) in which God gave form to everything which is not Him. Therefore, the terms employed by ᶜAbd al-Kader in this phrase include at the same time the domain of informal manifestation and the domain of supersensible formal

manifestation. These degrees, although they are superior to those of gross manifestation, are nonetheless themselves devoid of all reality with respect to the Absolute being and thus constitute yet other "temptations" for the spiritual man.

9. Concerning the notions of *jadhba* and of *sulūk*, see our introduction p. 9.

10. This perilous aspect of the initiatic voyage is more particularly treated by Ibn ʿArabī in his *Risālat al-anwār* (Hayderabad, 1948), see especially p. 9–13; and in the commentary on it attributed to ʿAbd al-Karīm al-Jīlī (Damascus, 1329 A.H., 129ff.). An English translation of this work, with extracts of the commentary, was published under the title *Journey to the Lord of Power* (New York, 1981), by R. Terri Harris.

11. This refers to Ibn ʿAṭā Allāh (d. 1309), the third Shaikh of the Shādhilite brotherhood, whose "Sentences" (*Ḥikam*) summarizes with great conciseness and force the fundamental rules of the Way. There is a French edition and translation of the *Ḥikam* by P. Nwyia: *Ibn ʿAṭā Allāh et la Naissance de la confrérie shādhilite* (Beirut, 1972); and an English translation by Victor Danner: Ibn ʿAṭā Allāh, *The Book of Wisdom* (New York, 1978). The text cited by the Amir, from memory and not literally, is that of sentence 19 (for the exact text, see Nwyia, *op. cit.*, 95).

12. *Murād*: traditionally this term is opposed to the term *murīd* ("one who desires") which, in the vocabulary of Sufism, designates the disciple who undertakes the initiatic voyage. Desire and will are "torn away" or "removed" from the *murād* (this definition is taken by ʿAbd al-Kader from Ibn ʿArabī, Kitāb Iṣṭilāḥ al-Sūfiyya, Hayderabad, 1948, (hereafter cited as *Ist.*), definition 4) while the *murīd* makes an effort to try to remove them from himself (cf. ibid., definition 3). In any case, while the first of these terms corresponds to an objective reality, the second simply translates the subjective perception which the initiate has of his own spiritual situation. As the masters abundantly emphasize, there is no *murīd* who was not first of all *murād*; desired by God.

13. Concerning contraction (*qabḍ*), see note 182.

14. The word *awzājan*, which we translate as "groups," properly designates "couples" or "pairs" and must be understood esoterically as an allusion to the situation of beings who live in the world of duality without perceiving its illusory character.

15. It is quite probable that the "servant" in question is none other than ᶜAbd al-Kader himself. This mode of indirect expression to relate an inner spiritual event is used quite frequently by the masters of *taṣawwuf.* Ibn ᶜArabī uses it on many occasions.

16. "Am I not your Lord?" This is an allusion to the "primordial Pact" (*mīthāq*) described in Kor. 7:172, whereby, in response to this question, all men to come until the end of time recognize the divine Lordship. It was this evidence of the Lordship which every being perceived and confessed when he was still "in the loins of Adam" which is the basis of the validity of the "Bearing Witness" (*shahāda*) demanded of each Muslim (*lā ilāha illa Llāh,* "there is no god but Allāh"): for one can only bear witness to what one has seen, and the *shahāda* is not a simple "act of faith." Thus the essential object of spiritual discipline, according to the masters of *taṣawwuf,* is to reactualize this original evidence, and the initiatic pact (*ᶜahd, mubāyaᶜa*) with the Shaikh is nothing other than a renewal and a confirmation of the primordial Pact.

17. See note 55 for the *ḥadīth* to which this phrase alludes.

18. Concerning the jinn, see note 56.

19. The "sacred Mosque" (*al-masjid al-ḥaram*) designates the Mosque at Mecca, at the center of which is the Kaᶜaba. The *maṭāf* is the space arranged for the ritual circumambulation (*ṭawāf*), outside of which it is not valid. The spiritual event described in this chapter probably took place in the course of a sojourn which the Amir made to the Ḥijāz between January 1863 and July 1864.

20. Concerning this "projection" of a verse of the revelation, see text 36.

21. *Imām al-Ḥaramayn,* is the honorary name of the theologian Abū l-Maᶜālī ᶜAbd al-Malik al-Juwanī (1028–1085).

22. The opinions mentioned in this paragraph—briefly summarized—are those of the principal theological schools concerning the problem of "the attribution of acts" (which the Amir treats more fully in text 32). A study in depth of this problem has been made by M. Daniel Gimaret in his thesis, *Théories de l'acte humain en théologie musulmane* (Paris 1980).

23. *Ḥukman lā ᶜaynan*: this extinction (*fanāʾ*) in God has the effect of making the creature lose the status of apparent autonomy which he possessed among the degrees of the universal Manifes-

tation but does not affect his essential reality which subsists eternally in the divine Knowledge in the form of the *ᶜayn thābita*, the "immutable prototype."

24. Allusion to the traditional hierarchy in Sufism of the degrees of certitude (inspired by Koran 102:5–7): *ᶜilm al-yaqīn*, the "knowledge of certitude," represents simple, theoretical knowledge; *ᶜayn al-yaqīn*, the "eye of certitude," corresponds to the knowledge which results from direct vision; *ḥaqq al-yaqīn*, the "reality of certitude," corresponds to the total identification of the knower and the known. These three terms are defined by Ibn ᶜArabī in *Ist.*, definitions 56, 57 and 58.

25. This phrase makes an implicit reference to a celebrated formulation of Ghazālī according to which this world is the most perfect of all the possible worlds. The Amir commented on this formula in M. 226 (p. 500–507 of the Arabic text) and in M. 369 (p. 1361–1370 of the Arabic text). The latter is in response to a question asked by the Shaikh Salīm alᶜAṭṭār (cf. *Tuḥfa*, vol. 2, p. 224). Ibn ᶜArabī also cited it several times (*Fut.* vol. 1, p. 259; vol. 3, p. 449, etc.)

26. Ibn ᶜArabī commented on the introductory verse of this chapter in *Fus.*, vol. 1, p. 92 (*Faṣṣ Ismāʾīl*).

27. Concerning Ibn ᶜAṭā Allāh, see note 11.

28. Concerning the significance of the term *laᶜalla* ("perhaps") in the divine discourse, see note 51.

29. The regularity of this lineage is expressed by the *silsila*, the "chain"—going back through an uninterrupted series of intermediaries to the Prophet himself—by which is transmitted the *baraka*, the spiritual influence. The function of the master (*murshid*, *shaikh*) obligatorily implies his attachment to one of these chains.

30. This phase refers to the technical notions belonging to the vocabulary of Islamic spiritual phenomonology. *Al-wārid*, inspiration, designates according to Ibn ᶜArabī (*Ist.*, definition 59) "all the praiseworthy thoughts which come unexpectedly into the heart without previous effort." *Al-barq*, lightning, is defined by Jurjānī (*Taᶜrifāt*, s.v.) as "the first manifestation to the servant of the brilliant flashes of the supersensible light; it invites him to penetrate into the place of the Proximity of the Lord with a view to 'the journey to Allāh.' " The *wāqiᶜa*, "the event," generally applies in *taṣawwuf* to a vision taking place between waking and sleep.

31. "Die before dying": reported by Tirmidhī, *qiyāma*, 25 (where the *ḥadīth* continues: " . . . and demand of yourself an accounting before an accounting is demanded of you.") This refers of course to the initiatic death without which there is no "second birth" and which is referred to in a Sufi adage tirelessly repeated through the centuries, prescribing to the disciple to be, in his relation to his Shaikh, "as a corpse in the hands of the washer of the dead." Certain masters institute, within the general notion of the initiatic death, a fourfold distinction: the "red" death corresponds to the combat against the passions, the "white" death corresponds to fasting, "the "green" death corresponds to the investiture of the *muraqqaᶜa* (the patchwork robe of the Sufis), the "black" death consists in seeing the acts of the creatures as coming from God alone. Ibn ᶜArabī deals with this symbolism in the *Kitāb al-amr al-muḥkam* and the *Kitāb kunh mā lā budda bi-l-murīd minhu* (c.f. Asin Palacios, *El Islam cristianizado* Madrid, 1931, 163). See also Jurjānī, *Taᶜrīfāt*, s.v.

32. The expression "new creation" (*khalq jadīd*) taken from Kor. 50:15 covers a fundamental idea of Ibn ᶜArabī (*Fus.*, vol. 1, p. 126, 156, *Fut.*, vol. 3, p. 189–199, etc.), that of the incessant renewal of the universe—whose continuity therefore is only apparent—by an inexhaustible play of theophanies of which it is only the theater. An exposition of this theme, and especially of its formulation by ᶜAyn al-Quḍāt al-Hamadānī (d. 525/1131), can be found in T. Izutsu, *Unicité de l'existence et Création perpetuelle en mystique islamique* (Paris, 1980), 96–120.

33. As indicated by the title—*al-qiyāma*—of the Sura which contains these verses, this Koranic text relates in the obvious sense to the Ressurection and the Last Judgment. The exoteric commentaries limit themselves to this interpretation. Following his usual method, which is that of Ibn ᶜArabī, ᶜAbd al-Kader does not in any way contest the validity of this interpretation in its own order but develops a microcosmic interpretation in which the phenomena mentioned by the Revelation are understood as spiritual events, marking out the itinerary of the gnostic. (Qāshānī also emphasizes, as is his custom, the microcosmic interpretation but situates these events at the moment of physical death, which is the "small resurrection," *al-qiyāmat al-sughra*).

34. In the Akbarian doctrine, the universe is nothing other than the inexhaustible succession of theophanies (*Fus.*, vol. 1, p. 81) and one cannot speak, for a particular individual, of the "moment when the theophanies begin." But it is one thing to know

that the world is only theophanies, and it is another thing to perceive the theophanies as such (this distinction corresponds to that used by certain authors like Jāmī between *tajallī wujūdī* and *tajallī shuhūdī* or *ᶜirfānī*). The spiritual event, the "resurrection" (*qiyāma*) which is referred to here, inaugurates this unveiling.

35. This definition of *maqām al-jamᶜ* is literally the same as that given by Ibn ʾArabī in *Ist.*, definition 37.

36. This phrase is taken from a *ḥadīth* where it applies to the Muslim survivors of the battle of Badr (Bukhārī, *maghāzi*, 9).

37. We translate freely this famous formula taken from the prophetic traditions (for example Bukhārī, *adāb*, 95) without which it would not be intelligible to the reader.

38. See note 81.

39. This *ḥadīth*, absent from the canonical collections, is often cited by Ibn ʾArabī (*Fus.*, vol. 1, p. 72–73; *Fut.*, vol. 1, p. 270–272; vol. 3, p. 490, etc.).

40. The *sunna* is the totality of the rules of conduct founded upon the words or the actions of the Prophet, and it is one of the sources of the sacred Law (*sharīᶜa*). As such it specifies the mode of application of many of the points in the prescriptions instituted in the Koranic revelations. This is the case with respect to the five legal prayers which are in question here. Each of these prayers comprises a variable number of sequences (*rakʾa*, pl. *rakʾat*). The prayer at dawn comprises two *rakʾ*as, during which the prescribed Koranic recitations are said in a loud voice. The prayers at midday and afternoon each comprise four *rakʾ*as, during which the Koranic recitations are done in a soft voice. In the prayer at sundown (3 *rakʾ*as) and the prayer at night (4 *rakʾ*as), the two first *rakʾ*as only are recited in a loud voice, the rest is said in a soft voice.

41. Concerning the *barzakh*, see note 129.

42. This expression appears in a *ḥadīth* reported among others by Muslim, *ḥajj*, 426.

43. The end of this sentence in the Arabic text is broken or distorted. We have reconstructed the most probable meaning.

44. The terms employed here should not be considered as simple stylistic figures of speech but as corresponding to the modalities, more or less luminous, of the theophanic unveilings.

45. Ibn ᶜArabī (*Fut.*, vol. 1, p. 395–396) treats the symbolism of the moments of the prayer in a slightly different way but it is also based on the correspondence between night and the world of non-manifestation (*ᶜālam al-ghayb*) on the one hand, and day and the world of manifestation (*ᶜālam al-shahāda*) on the other.

46. Concerning the three degrees of certitude, see note 24.

47. This "proof" at the degree symbolized by the expression *ᶜayn al-yaqin* is not of a rational indirect order, as in the preceding degree: it consists in the direct vision of the object of the certitude and that is why all doubt is excluded here. As for the "reality of the certitude," it corresponds to the identification of the knowing subject with the known object which leaves no place for proof since proof necessarily implies a duality which has here been transcended.

48. *Mulk, malakūt*: these two terms can be translated respectively as "kingdom" and "kingship." For Ibn ᶜArabī (*Ist.*, definitions 175, 176), as for the majority of authors, they designate the domain of manifestation (*ᶜālam al-shahāda*) and the domain of non-manifestation (*ᶜālam al-ghayb*).

49. The passive voice is—as its Arabic name indicates—the voice where the subject of the verb remains unknown (*majhūl*).

50. The end of the verse ("perhaps, etc.") is not given in the edition of the *Mawāqif*, even though it is referred to a few lines later. It was therefore necessary, for the comprehension of the text, to complete the quotation.

51. *Laᶜalla*, "perhaps," in spite of the character of doubt which it introduces into human discourse, should not, when it is God who speaks, be interpreted as the expression of an uncertainty about the occurrence of an event or the realization of a promise. This uncertainty would imply in effect an absurd metaphysical limitation on the divine knowledge in the first case and on the divine Justice or the divine Power in the second. Therefore, the commentators of the Koran recognize in the constructions of the type we are encountering here, according to the context, either the character of an affirmation or the character of an exhortation ("may you").

52. For the Amir and the school of Ibn ᶜArabī, the word *tawḥīd*, used here and in the following sentence, covers a plurality of hierarchically superimposed meanings, starting from its usual exoteric meaning (where it designates the simple verbal

affirmation that God is unique) up to the effective realization of the supreme Identity of the divine Self and the "me" of the servant. Its translation must then vary with the context.

53. The words *yattaqūn* and *ittiqā* both belong to the eighth verb form of the same root, WQY, which, depending on the case, expresses the idea of "fear" (more precisely "fear of God"), of "beware of" or of "protect." It is this last meaning which Ibn ʿArabī generally assumes. Consequently, he gives to verses analogous to the one commented upon here a somewhat different interpretation (for example, see *Fus.*, vol. 1, p. 56).

54. *Ḥuḍūr* can be translated as "concentration," but this translation fails to make clear the relation between this word and the verb from the same root, *istaḥḍarū* ("make present") which appears later in the text. To be present to God through the invocation has the effect, from the point of view of the servant, of "making God present," even though, metaphysically, one cannot speak in any case, or for any being, of an "absence of God."

55. This *hādīth* appears in several of the canonical collections, notably in Muslim (usual source of the Amir), *Ṣaḥīḥ*, *ṣalāt*, 148, 222; *dhikr*, 96.

56. The jinn, who are mentioned on many occasions in the Koran (6:128, 130; 7:179, p. 184; 11:119; 72 [the whole Sura]; 114:6, etc.), represent subtle entities of an igneous nature (*nāriyya*) in contrast to angels who are of a luminous nature (*nūriyya*). Ibn ʿArabī, who points out that this word can designate the inner psychic forces of man (*Fut.*, vol. 3, p. 354), on several occasions deals with the nature of the jinn: *Fut.*, vol. 1, p. 131–134; vol. 1, p. 272–273; vol. 3, p. 367.

57. The first "station of separation" (*maqam al-farq*) corresponds to the state of the ordinary man who perceives the universe as distinct from God. Starting from here, the initiatic itinerary leads the being first to extinction in the divine Unity, which abolishes all perception of created things. But spiritual realization, if it is complete, arrives afterwards at the "second station of separation" where the being perceives simultaneously the one in the multiple and the multiple in the one.

58. The negation is missing in the printed text which gives: *ʿinda l-asbāb wa bi-l-asbāb*. Its absence makes the phrase unintelligible and contradictory to the other statements by the Amir—and by Ibn ʿArabī—on the same subject.

59. "No soul will profit from its faith . . ." The completion of the verse specifies " . . . if it has not believed before." In its obvious sense, the verse relates to the appearance of the "signs of the Hour," which will announce the end of the world, among which, according to the *ḥadīth* which the text will mention in the following line, will be "the rising of the sun at the place where it sets," that is to say, in the west (Tirmidhī, *fitan*, 22). The "gate of repentance" will then be closed and for those who have lived in infidelity it will be too late to profess the true faith.

60. See text 25 for a commentary on this "verse of Light."

61. Cf. note 98bis. ᶜAbd al-Kader, who comments on this formula in M. 48 (p. 101 of the Arabic text) evokes in M. 163 the controversies relative to its attribution to the Prophet without expressing a decision about it.

62. Concerning the *tawba*, see text 35 and note 176.

63. Allusion to Kor. 57:4 which ᶜAbd al-Kader comments upon in M. 132, here text 19.

64. One should correct *ᶜadl*, which the printed text contains, to *ᶜadam*.

65. Allusion to Kor. 18:77 and 18:82, but with the notable difference that with the same goal—to preserve the treasure for those for whom it is destined—Khaḍir receives from God the order to *reconstruct* the wall.

66. *Ma anta?* not *Man anta?* as it was previously.

67. This sentence, often cited with slight variations, is attributed to Sahl Tustarī (203/818–283/896). On its interpretation, cf. *Fut.*, vol. 1, p. 42–43.

68. Limited to its first part, this formulation is in fact metaphysically correct in the perspective of the *waḥdat al-wujūd*. If it can, under certain conditions, as we will see, legitimately expose the one who pronounces it to a punishment in this life, it cannot involve him in a posthumous punishment. It is the addition of the stipulation "apart from Him" which, by introducing duality onto the plane of pure Unitude, transforms this affirmation into an absurdity, therefore a blasphemy, and justifies the infernal pains mentioned in the verse.

69. Concerning Ḥallāj and the circumstances of his condemnation see L. Massignon, *Passion*, I, p. 385–606.

70. Abū Yazīd al-Bisṭāmī, one of the great saints of the first centuries of Islam (d. 234/857 or 261/874), of whom are reported some "ecstatic sayings" (*shataḥāt*) which, from the point of view of exotericism, are no less "scandalous" than those of Ḥallāj.

71. This final part of a formula of invocation utilized by the Prophet is found with some variations in several canonical collections, for example, the *Ṣaḥīḥ* of Bukhārī, *daᶜawāt*, 10.

72. Concerning the significance of this allusion to the divine Name *al-Nur* (the Light), see text 25 which comments on the "verse of Light."

73. Concerning the meaning of this variant, see the beginning of text 18 which comments a second time on this Koranic verse.

74. Concerning the *aᶜyān thābita*, see note 128.

75. Concerning the problem of attribution of acts and its Koranic sources, see text 32 and 33 and note 22.

76. The symbolism of the Light, whose effusion makes the things of non-being (*al-ᶜadam*) pass to being (*al-wujūd*), is treated in text 25.

77. The *Huwa*, which refers to the third person of discourse is, according to its usual definition, the "pronoun of the absent person." The unfolding of the metaphysical implications of the grammar of a sacred language—whose rules are divinely instituted and do not come from simple human convention—constitutes one of the traditional ways of the esoteric hermenuetic of the Revelation. The Amir—following Ibn ᶜArabī—has recourse to it. A characteristic example is offered by text 32.

78. This quotation is a *ḥadīth* reported several times in the canonical collections (for example, Bukhārī, *Ṣaḥīḥ*, *manāqib al-Anṣār*, 36; *adab*, 90). In its complete form it specifies further the name of the poet who is alluded to: it was Labid, author of one of the seven *muᶜallaqāt*.

79. These relations, in fact, do not in any way modify the respective ontological status of the terms between which they are established: to say of a man that he is a lion does not make him a lion, nor the lion a man.

80. This specification is necessary in order to distinguish the esoteric interpretation of a verse from its usual interpretation by the exoteric commentators for whom Allāh is only "with us" by His knowledge. This problem is discussed a little further on.

81. These terms designate in Muslim dogmatics so many heretical doctrines often imputed—incorrectly—to the Shaikh al-Akbar and his school by the polemicists. These attacks, of which the long lists established by M. Osman Yahya show the extent and the persistence through the centuries (see on this subject his *Histoire et Classification de l'oeuvre d'Ibn ᶜArabī,* [Damascus, 1964], 1, p. 114–132; and his introduction to *Naṣṣ al-nuṣūṣ* of Ḥaydar Āmulī [Teheran], 1975, p. 36–62 of the Arabic text), still continue today; notably in Egypt where, several years ago, the orthodoxy of Ibn ᶜArabī was the object of a violent press campaign and of debates in Parliament. Indeed these debates arrived at a decision—today lifted—to forbid the appearance of the critical edition of the *Futūḥāt* which is currently in the process of publication. The majority of themes of the anti-Akbarian polemic were already found in the work of Ibn Taymiyya (1263–1328) and in particular in his *Risāla ilā man saʾalahu ᶜan haqīqati madhhab al-ittiḥadiyyīn (Majmūᶜat al-rasāʾil,* edition Rashīd Riḍā, 5, p. 1–102).

82. Thus, they cannot, by this reductive interpretation, "safeguard," as they intend, the divine transcendence.

83. Concerning the notion of "face" see text 23.

84. This notion and the correlative one of the "Proximity by supererogatory works" (*qurb al-nawāfil*) are fundamental for Ibn ᶜArabī and have methodological consequences in the initiatic teachings which have been marked by his influence. They are both based on a *ḥadīth qudsī* often cited and commented upon in the literature of *taṣawwuf.* We give here the text as it was given by Bukhārī (*Bāb al-tawāḍuᶜ*) following Abū Hurayra: "The Messenger of God—On him be Grace and Peace!—said: 'God said, "He who treats one of my friends (or 'one of My saints'—*walī*) as an enemy, upon him I declare war. My servant does not approach Me with anything that I love more than the works that I have prescribed for him. And he does not cease to approach Me through supererogatory works until I love him. And when I love him, I am the hearing by which he hears, the sight by which he sees, the hand with which he takes hold, the foot with which he walks. If he asks of Me, I give to him; if he seeks refuge in Me, I protect him. I never hesitate to do anything as much as I hesitate to take the soul of the believer who hates death, for I hate to do him harm.'" Ibn ᶜArabī, who includes this *ḥadīth* in a collection of *ḥadīth*-s *qudsi*-s, of which he is the author, the *Mishkāt al-anwār,* cites and comments upon the central part of this *ḥadīth* repeatedly in the *Futūḥāt Makkiyya* (see for example vol. 1, p. 406; vol. 3, p. 68; vol. 4, p. 20, 24, 30). By the

practice of the *nawāfil,* the supererogatory acts of piety, the servant approaches Allāh to the point where he hears, sees, takes hold through Him: at the same time, this "substitution" of Allāh for the servant is not limited to the external senses but according to Ibn ʿArabī also extends to the internal faculties. It is therefore total: Allāh is the very being of the servant. On the other hand, the Shaikh al-Akbar emphasizes (*Fut.*, vol. 1, p. 406) that one must not think that, in this occurrence, anything new is produced: Allāh has *always* been the hearing, the sight, etc. and it was only the veil of illusion that prevented the servant from being conscious of this. The practice of the *nawāfil* has simply resulted in a *kashf,* an "unveiling," which has made him discover the permanent reality which he was ignorant of. The "proximity" in question is nothing other, in fact, than an allusion to the supreme Identity, that of the *Ḥaqq* (the divine Reality) with the *Khalq* (the creature).

Nevertheless, this "station," as the Amir points out, is not, for Ibn ʿArabī, the most perfect (cf. *Fut.*, vol. 4, p. 24, 449). If, in the *qurb al-nawāfil* (obtained by the practice of supererogatory acts, where by definition the will of the creature plays a part), Allāh hears, sees . . . in the place of the servant, correlatively, in the *qurb al-farāʾiḍ* (which the creature attains by manifesting his absolute servitude—that is to say, his radical ontological indigence—by the accomplishment of obligatory acts, where his own will is totally extinguished), *it is, on the contrary, the servant who "becomes" the hearing, the sight and hand of Allāh.*

These two "proximities" are in the same hierarchical relation as the *Nawāfil* and the *Farāʾiḍ* (the *Farāʾiḍ* play the role of principal with respect to the *Nawāfil*; cf. *Fut.*, vol. 1., p. 203) and correspond respectively to the "ascending" realization and the "descending" realization as they are described in chapter 45 of *Futūḥāt.* (A translation and commentary of this chapter have been given by M. Vālsan in an article of the magazine *Etudes traditionnelles* [April–May 1952], under the title "Un texte du Cheikh al-Akbar sur la 'realisation descendante'.") Let us note in passing that one catches a glimpse here of the profound significance of a celebrated definition which Ibn ʿArabī recalls at the end of chapter 25 of the *Futūḥāt,* commenting that "under these words is hidden an immense science," and according to which the *taṣawwuf* consists of the "five prayers and the expectation of death."

85. This verse is part of an episode in the Koran—which corresponds to an episode in the Talmud—in the course of which Abraham is thrown by idolaters into a furnace out of which, thanks to divine intervention, he escapes intact.

86. These terms allude to Koranic verses concerning Abraham which are cited a little further on.

87. An allusion to the celebrated *ḥadīth*—which refers to the *Ḥaqīqa muḥamadiyya*, the metahistorical "Muhammadan Reality," and not the historical person of the Prophet—according to which "I was Prophet when Adam was still between the water and the mud." (Bukhārī, *adāb*, 119) Ibn ᶜArabī has commented on many occasions upon the doctrinal implications of this notion according to which the "Seal of the Prophets," who closes the cycle of prophethood, is also the original source of all prophethood. (See for example *Fus.*, vol. 1, p. 63ff.; *Fut.*, vol. 1, p. 243.)

87bis. This identification with Abraham is affirmed by the Koranic text itself (Kor. 14:36) in which Abraham declares: "He who follows me, he in truth is part of me (*fa-innahu minnī*)."

88. It should be understood that God did not limit Himself to saying that he made everything from water but specified: "every living thing." Now, that which makes something "living" is the presence in it of the spirit which proceeds from the "Breath of the Merciful." Therefore, only the form of the thing is made from water.

89. For Ibn ᶜArabī (cf. *Fus.*, vol. 1, 143–144) the "Breath of the Merciful" is the *hayūlā* (from the Greek *hylé*), the materia prima of the "divine words" (*kalimāt*). Now, all created beings, considered in relation to their essential reality (*ḥaqīqa*), not in relation to their form (*ṣūra*), are "words of God" (*Fut.*, vol. 2, p. 366, 400, 402, 404, etc.).

90. Ibn ᶜArabī often insists, starting from the same scriptural arguments or other similar ones, on the fact that there is nothing in the universal Manifestation, envisaged in all its degrees and all its modalities that is not living. Therefore, there is no place in the Akbarian doctrine for an "inert" material or an "inanimate" object (*Fus.*, vol. 1, p. 179; *Fut.*, vol. 3, p. 258, etc.).

91. From which it results that accidents should by definition be said to be existent even if, because of the fact that their existence is subordinated to the existence of substance, they are situated at the lowest degree of the ontological hierarchy.

92. An allusion to a long *ḥadīth* on the posthumous states of the human being that Shaᶜrānī (Mukhtaṣar tadhkirat al-Qurtubī, Alep, 1395 h, p. 46) cites following Ibn Ḥanbal.

93. Cf. Shaʿrānī, op. cit., 116. This regeneration by the water of Life concerns the sinners from among the believers who, after having expiated their sins in Gehenna, will leave to enter paradise (Bukhārī, *tawḥīd*, 24/5).

94. This *ḥadīth* does not appear in the canonical collections and, according to the external criteria of authentication proper to the science of *ḥadīth*, is considered apocryphal even though for the majority of Sufis and notably Ibn ʿArabī it is validated by intuitive unveiling (*kashf*). Concerning this form of validation cf. *Fut.*, vol. 1, p. 150. For Ibn ʿArabī, this precious stone, which is more precisely a "white pearl" (*durra bayḍā*), is identical to the first intellect (*al-ʿaql al-awwal*; *Ist.*, definition 118; *Fut.*, vol. 1, p. 46), which is one of the designations of the "Muhammadan Reality," The Shaikh al-Akbar states (*ʿUqlat al-mustawfiz.*, ed. Nyberg, p. 56) that he has devoted a special treatise to the *durra bayḍā*.

95. On the "Muhammadan Reality" (*al-ḥaqiqa al-muḥammadiyya*), see note 129.

96. The four elements—including the element water—thus represent so many differentiations of the primordial water, whose role here corresponds to that of ether (*ākāsha*) in the Hindu tradition.

97. The *Lām-Alif* (لا), although it is formed from the combination of the two letters, is often considered an autonomous letter by the Arabic authors, thus adding to the 28 which normally make up the alphabet. Concerning the symbolism of the *Lām-Alif* (treated here by the Amir essentially in its graphic aspect but which, because of its grammatical function, also raises other very interesting considerations), see *Fut.*, vol. 1, 75–78 in which Ibn ʿArabī treats the relations between the *Lām-Alif* (which pronounced *Lā*, is a negative particle) and the *Alif-Lām* (which, pronounced *Al*, is the definite article in Arabic.) See also *Fut.* vol. 1, p. 177, which can be compared with the first redaction by consulting the critical edition of O. Yahya, vol. 3, p. 134; as well as *Fut.*, vol. 2, p. 123, in which Ibn ʿArabī responds to question 141 of the questionaire of Tirmidhī. The edition of the *Khatm al-awilyāʾ* of M. Osman Yahya (Beirut, 1965), 312 in a footnote, also gives a different formulation of this same response taken from another treatise of the Shaikh al-Akbar, the *Jawāb Mustaqīm*.

98. We are filling in here a lacuna of the printed text which omits repeating "*al-wujūd al-ḥaqq*" which the context requires.

98bis. Cf. note 61. This famous formula, one often cited by the masters of *taṣawwuf,* is generally considered a *ḥadīth nabawī,* that is, a saying attributed to the Prophet, or even as a *ḥadīth qudsī* (in which the Prophet reports a saying in which God expresses himself in the first person). Some authors believe that this is an apocryphal *ḥadīth,* and attribute this sentence to Yaḥya b. Muᶜādh al-Rāzī (d. 258/871) (cf. Massignon, *Lexique technique* Paris, 1954, p. 127). Ibn ᶜArabī—who always cites it in the form *man ᶜarafa nafsahu ᶜarafa rabbahu* (without *qad*)—considers it to be a *ḥadīth nabawī* (see *Fut.*, vol. 1, p. 328, p. 331, p. 353; vol. 2, p. 297, etc.). One must remember at this point that the treatise entitled "*Risāla fī l-aḥadiyya*" or "*Risāla wujūdiyya,* published several times and translated (by ᶜAbd al-Hādī into French and by T.H. Weir into English) under the name of Ibn ᶜArabī, and which is presented as an esoteric commentary on this *ḥadīth,* is in reality by Awḥad al-dīn Balyānī (d. 686/1287) who, through his master Shustarī, was connected to the spiritual lineage of Ibn Sabᶜīn. This connection, both initiatic and doctrinal, explains the marked divergences of this commentary from akbarian interpretations.

99. Concerning the difference between progressive spiritual realization, which is that of the *sālik,* and that which results from an "ecstatic rapture" (*jadhb*), see our introduction p. 9.

100. *Al-Ḥaqq* (God) is omitted in the printed text.

101. For the Amir, the two terms, *waḥdat al-wujūd* and *waḥdat al-shuhūd,* often opposed to each other in polemics which we cannot analyze here, represent two complementary aspects of the spiritual realization. In particular he explains it in M. 192 (*Mawāqif,* p. 419–421). See also our introduction p. 16.

102. We should not forget that the term "union," even if it has a certain subjective and psychological validity, is metaphysically improper as the author often emphasizes. For example, see text 19.

103. In order to understand the text, we need to cite the preceding verse of Sura 55: "Every being upon it (the earth) perishes. Only the Face of your Lord subsists . . . " This "Face" or the divine aspect proper to each being—identical to the "something uncreated and uncreatable" spoken of by Meister Eckhart—constitutes, in the doctrine of the Shaikh al-Akbar and his school the metaphysical foundation of the creature; the "Lord" being, for each creature, the particular divine Name of which it is the

"epiphanic place." It is for this reason that Ibn ᶜArabī, when he comments (for example in *Fut.*, vol. 3, p. 420) upon verse 28:88, "Everything perishes except His face" (where the possessive pronoun is generally interpreted as relating to God), considers that this refers to the "face" of the thing. In any case, these two interpretations are only contradictory in appearance.

104. The word *sirr,* plural *asrār,* which we will encounter again later in the text, is, in the vocabulary of sacred anthropology, one of the designations of the center of the being and in this sense is identified with the heart (*qalb*). It can, however, in some cases, take on a more precise technical meaning in relation to the localization of the different subtle centers which the initiatic discipline has the aim of awakening. Concerning the notion of *wajh* see H. Corbin, *Face de Dieu, face de l'homme,* Paris 1983, pp. 237–295 (where this akbarian theme is treated with special reference to shiᶜīte texts).

105. An allusion to a famous *ḥadīth qudsī* ("My heaven and My earth cannot contain Me, but the heart of My faithful servant contains Me") often cited in the literature of *Taṣawwuf* with an *isnād* going back to Wahb b. Munabbīh, but which does not appear in the canonical collections.

106. The *qibla* is the direction of the sacred Mosque (of Mecca), which is cited in the introductory verse, toward which the worshipper should turn when he performs the ritual prayers.

107. This is not a citation from the Koran, but is from a *ḥadīth qudsī* (Ibn Ḥanbal, *Musnad,* II, 404; Muslim, *Ṣaḥīḥ, birr,* 43). This is the continuation of the *ḥadīth* (to be compared with Matthew 25:41–45): [The man answers:] "O my Lord, how can I visit You, since You are the Lord of the worlds?" God said: "Did you not know that one of my servants was sick? And still you did not visit him! Did you not know that, if you had visited him, you would have found Me with him?" The dialogue continues in this same manner. This text, in which the divine "I" identifies itself with the very being of the creature, is commented upon by Ibn ᶜArabī in *Fut.,* vol. 1, p. 407, which also cites the *ḥadīth qudsī* according to which "I am his hearing, his sight, etc." (see note 84) which the Amir mentions in the subsequent line.

108. In other words: it is the presence in man (and in every being) of this divine "face" which justifies the identification which the texts establish between the *Ḥaqq* and the *Khalq.*

109. See the commentary on this verse in text 28.

110. See note 81.

111. For this is the proper sense of the word *masjid,* usually translated by the word "mosque."

112. This is the response given by a Shaikh of Abādān to Sahl b. ᶜAbdallāh al-Tustarī (d. 283/896). Ibn ᶜArabī, who often evokes this episode (*Fut.,* vol. 2, p. 20, 32, 34, 102; vol. 3, p. 302–308), states that the "prostration of the heart" (*sujūd al-qalb*) is an extremely rare modality of spiritual realization but that Sahl had experienced it from the time he was six and searched in vain for a long time for a master who could instruct him concerning his state. This episode in the life of Sahl is quite probably that evoked in the *Risāla qushayriyya* (Cairo, 1957), p. 15. The name of the Shaikh in question would therefore be Abū Ḥabīb Ḥamza b. ᶜAbdallāh al-ᶜAbādānī.

113. An allusion to verse 3 of Sura 85 which begins with a triple oath, of which this is the last.

114. This formula appears in Tirmidhī (*imān,* 15) but, unless we are mistaken, it is not found in the *Ṣāḥīḥ* of Bukhārī.

115. In the Koranic verse, 57:20, the word *kuffār* (plural of *kāfir*) is used in the sense of "sowers" and the rest of the phrase undoubtedly alludes to this.

116. An allusion to three sentences attributed to the first Caliphs. The first is: "I never see a thing without seeing Allāh *before* that thing." The second is: "I never see a thing without seeing Allāh *at the same time* as that thing." The third is: "I never see a thing without seeing Allāh *after* the thing."

117. The affirmation that *tanzīh* and *tashbīh* are indissolubly linked in the supreme Knowledge is one of the characteristic themes of the akbarian doctrine. In particular, it is developed in the *Fuṣūṣ al-Ḥikam* (*Faṣṣ Nūḥ*).

118. We are inserting the divine name *al-ẓāhir,* which is omitted in the printed text, but which the sense requires.

119. Concerning this *ḥadīth,* see text 23 and note 107.

120. "Those who make a pact with you . . ." The "you" of this verse, as the "you" of the verse cited subsequently, designates the Prophet.

121. See text 36 and note 183.

122. This paragraph on Abū Saʿīd al-Kharrāz is a shortened form of a passage from the *Fuṣūṣ,* vol. 1, p. 77.

123. It is impossible to translate the last phrase, in which the text is obviously distorted or corrupted.

124. This famous Koranic verse has evoked innumerable commentaries, the best known of which is undoubtedly the one which Ghazālī (1058–1111) wrote entitled *Mishkāt al-Anwār,* edited by ʿAfīfī (Cairo, 1964). An excellent French translation of the treatise by R. Deladriere, entitled *Le Tabernacle des Lumières* was published by Editions du Seuil, (Paris, 1980).

On the interpretation of this same verse by Ibn ʿArabī, refer to the article by Denis Gril, "Le commentaire du verset de la Lumière d'après Ibn ʿArabī, *Bulletin d'etudes orientales,* vol. 29, (Damascus, 1977), p. 179–189 (In addition to the numerous texts which he cites, there is a brief but interesting reference in the commentary to *Tarjumān al-Ashwāq,* edited in Beirut, 1961, p. 17).

125. *Al-Nūr* is one of the 99 divine Names.

126. Concerning the "need" which the divine Names have of the creatures in order to manifest themselves, cf. *Fus.,* p. 111–112.

127. In *Fut.,* vol. 1,p. 101, Ibn ʿArabī writes: "Each divine Name contains all the others and is qualified by all the others." He says further in *Fus.,* vol. 1, p. 79, that "Inasmuch as each divine Name designates the Essence, all the Names belong [to each divine Name] but inasmuch as each divine Name designates the particular sense which is proper to it, it is distinct from the others."

128. *Thubut,* permanence, stability, means to Ibn ʿArabī the mode of presence of the possibles in the divine Knowledge. "The possibles have immutable essences—or prototypes, *aʿyān,* devoid of any being of their own, which accompany the Necessary Being in eternity." (*Fut.,* vol. 3, p. 429) "There is no form that exists which is not identical to its own immutable prototype; being is upon it as a garment." (*Fut.,* vol. 1, p. 302) "That which you were in your state of *thubūt,* you manifest in your existence, to the extent that you can affirm your existence." (*Fus.,* vol. 1, p. 83)

129. The "Muhammadan reality" (*al-ḥaqīqa al-muḥammadiyya*) is defined by Ibn ʿArabī as follows: "At the beginning of the creation, there was the primordial dust (*al-habāʾ*). The first thing which was existentiated was the *Ḥaqīqa Muḥammadiyya . . .* Why was it

existentiated? In order to manifest the essential divine realities (*al-ḥaqāʾiq al-ilāhiyya*)." (*Fut.*, vol. 1, p. 118) See also *Fus.*, vol. 1, p. 63–64. The isthmus (*barzakh*) is for Ibn ʿArabī that which at the same time separates and joins two things, two orders of reality. The Prophet is the "Perfect Man," the "Universal Man" (*al-insān al-kāmil*) who is "an isthmus between the world and God, reuniting the creature and the Creator; he is the line of separation between the divine degree and the degree of existentiated things, similar to the line which separates the shadow from the sun." (*Inshā al-dawāʾir*, ed. Nyberg, p. 22) "He manifests himself with the divine Names, and in this respect he is God; and he also manifests himself with the nature of the contingents, and in this respect he is creature" (*Fut.*, vol. 2, p. 391).

130. We have omitted here two parts of the sentence which repeat literally the explanation of the symbolism of the glass and the niche as it appears several lines above. *Al-nūr al-wujūdī al-iḍāfī:* this light represents in fact a determination of the absolute Light which is that of the Essence, in which any kind of multiplicity—including that of the Names—is inconceivable.

131. This refers to Abū-l Qāsim b. ʿAbbād (fourth/tenth century), vizier of several Buyid Sultans and man of letters, not to be confused with Abū ʿAbdallāh Muḥammad b. ʿAbbād al-Rundī (eighth/fourteenth century), best known as a commentator of the *Ḥikam* of Ibn ʿAṭā Allāh. These verses are generally attributed to Abū Nuwās (d. circa 200/815). Ibn ʿAbrabī cites them—without attribution—in *Fut.* vol. 1, p. 64 and in his *Kitāb al-tajalliyāt*, Hayderabad, 1948, p. 43.

132. We have given a literal translation of this part of the sentence whose meaning has escaped us.

133. All symbolism implies, in effect, a relation between the symbol and that which it symbolizes. The divine Names can therefore be symbolized since they are the terms of a relation (no *rabb* without *marbūb*, etc.) But the Name Allāh, which contains them all in synthetic mode, is a Name of the Essence (*ism al-dhāt*) whose absolute transcendence excludes any relation with anything whatever and therefore excludes any symbolization.

134. "Predisposition" (*istiʿdād*, pl. *istiʿdādāt*) is a technical term used frequently by Ibn ʿArabī to signify the aptitude of the *aʿyān thābita*, the "immutable prototypes" contained in the divine Knowledge, for receiving—and thus for determining by the limi-

tations proper to each of them—the perpetual effusion (*fayḍ*) of the theophanies (see *Fus.*, vol. 1, p. 49, 59–60 and the commentaries of ᶜAffīfī, vol. 2, p. 21–23).

135. Cf. Ibn ᶜArabī, *Fus.*, vol. 1, p. 81: "The universe is nothing other than His theophany [conditioned] by the forms of the *aᶜyān thābita*."

136. For Ibn ᶜArabī (cf. *Fus.*, vol. 1 p. 82, 83) the Will of Allāh is exercised in conformity with what His Knowledge reveals to Him concerning the nature of the possibles. "It is not," writes the Shaikh al-Akbar, "the knowledge which acts on its object, but its object which acts on the knowledge." This is yet another confirmation of the perfect identity of views between ᶜAbd al- Kader and the author of the *Fuṣūṣ*. Indeed, it leads the Amir to refute (M. 346, in particular p. 1115) the critique which Jīlī (*Insān kāmil* (Cairo, 1388/1949), I, p. 46) addressed to Ibn ᶜArabī on this very point (M. 346, referred to above, also contains the description of a vision of Ibn ᶜArabī on p. 1114).

137. The divine order is to give alms "to the poor" (*li-l-fuqarāʾ*) with no other specification and thus does not impose any limitation on the choice of the recipient of the alms other than that he should belong to this very general category.

138. On the justification of this point of view, see text 21 and note 90.

139. This "minaret," or this "beacon" (*manār*), represents, for each divine Name, the place where its light manifests itself, the receptacle of its epiphany (cf *Fut.*, vol. 4, p. 327).

140. Ibn ᶜArabī, for whom "Allāh is the Worshipped in everything which is worshipped" (*Fut.*, vol. 2, p. 303), always interprets verse 17:31 in this way (eg. *Fut.*, vol. 1, p. 405).

141. The negation required by the meaning is omitted in the Arabic text.

142. According to a sentence attributed to Abū l-Ḥassan al-Shādhilī (d. 656/1258): "Allāh has effaced everything 'other than Him' by His saying: 'I am the First and the Last, the Apparent and the Hidden.' "

143. An allusion to a *ḥadīth qudsī*: "I am in conformity with the opinion which my servant has of Me" (Ibn Ḥanbal, *musnad*, 2, 391; Bukhārī, *tawhīd*, 15). This *ḥadīth* is interpreted in the same

way by Ibn ᶜArabī (see for example, *Fus.*, vol. 1, p. 226). Concerning "the god created in the beliefs" see also *Fut.*, vol. 4, p. 143, 279; and Corbin, *Imagination Creatrice*, p. 145–148.

144. On line 15 of page 768 of the Arabic text, it seems necessary to correct a copying error by deleting *ka-dhālika wa bi-khilāfī dhālika taᶜālā* and adding *annahu.*

145. It is the angels who are speaking in this verse.

146. This paradoxical phrase should not be interpreted, of course, as signifying that God does not know Himself, but as signifying that His Knowledge, which is an attribute of the Essence, cannot logically "contain" the latter, with which it is coextensive. Ibn ᶜArabī, in the next to last line of a passage whose theme is the same as that of this chapter of the *Mawāqif* (*Fus.*, vol. 1, p. 226), states concerning this very point in the most rigorous way: "One cannot say of a thing either that it contains itself or that it does not contain itself."

147. Concerning the nature of the esoteric meanings which the *ᶜārif bi-Llāh* can perceive in the revelation and their relations with the exoteric commentaries which deal with the obvious sense of the Koranic verses, see note 33, and the beginning of text 36. The distinction between showing the "subtle allusions" (*ishārāt*) and commentary properly speaking (*tafsīr*) is often affirmed by Ibn ᶜArabī. In the chapter of the *Futūḥāt* specifically devoted to the *ishārāt* (*Fut.*, vol. 1, p. 278), Ibn ᶜArabī emphasizes the fact that spiritual men do not designate as *tafsīr* the interpretation which they "see in themselves" (*mā yarawnahu fī nufūsihim*). This not only corresponds to a difference in nature between two modes of intellection, but it also serves as a measure of prudence to avoid controversies with the "literalists" (*ṣāḥib al-rusūm*).

148. The Arabic text gives the terms *nuzūl, inzāl, tanzīl, ītāʾ* which, although they have certain differences of meaning, are often used interchangeably to designate the "descent" of the Revelation.

149. This degree is that of the Name *Allāh* insofar as it applies to the *ulūhiyya*, the "function of divinity" (and not insofar as it applies to the divine Essence, which is "anterior" to the distinction of the Names).

150. The *ḥadīth* evoked here is that, reported in most of the canonical collections (for example, Bukhārī, *tawḥīd*, 35, *daᶜawāt*, 13, etc.) according to which: "Each night, Our Lord descends to

the heaven of this lower world, where He remains only during the last third of the night and says: 'Is there someone who invokes Me, that I may respond to him? Is there someone who addresses a prayer to Me, that I may answer it? Is there someone who asks me for pardon, that I may pardon him?'"

151. This phrase alludes to verse 31 of Sura 9 where it is said of the Christians: "They have taken their doctors and their monks, along with Jesus, son of Mary, as Lords alongside of Allāh." For ᶜAbd al-Kader, the "error" of the Christians is relative and not absolute. It does not consist in the fact of recognizing the created beings as manifestations of the divine Names, but in the reductive identification of God with one or another of His theophanies. The same remark is valid in reference to the Jews, envisaged in the following phrases, where the reference is to Kor. 9:30. This interpretation of "infidelity" (*kufr*) is analogous to that which Ibn ᶜArabī gives in the *Fuṣūṣ* with respect to Jesus (*Fus.*, vol. 1, p. 141) where he says that the error of the Christians does not reside in the affirmation that "Jesus is God" nor that "He is the son of Mary," but in the fact of "enclosing" (*taḍmin*) the vivifying power of God in the human person of Jesus.

152. According to a *ḥadīth* (Ibn Ḥanbal, 3, 145) the Muḥammadan community is divided into 71 or 73 sects.

153. This remark should be understood as follows: just as the Prophet Muḥammad is the "Seal of Prophethood," to whom "the knowledge of the first and the last" was given, so his community—in the person of its spiritual elite—inherits, by reason of its function at the end of the human cycle, the privilege of recapitulating, and thus validating, all the modes of knowledge of God corresponding to the specific perspectives of previous revelations.

154. *Al-muhayyamūn*: these "spirits lost in love," identified in the Muslim tradition with the Cherubim, are not, properly speaking, "angels," that is, "messengers." According to Ibn ᶜArabī (*Fut.*, vol. 2, p. 250), Allāh, when He existentiated them, epiphanized Himself to them through His Name *al-Jamīl* (the Beautiful), and this theophany "intoxicated" them. In this spiritual state of "extinction" (*fanāʾ*), they did not know "either themselves, nor Him whom they loved beyond all reason." The order addressed to the angels to prostrate themselves before Adam does not concern them (see *Fut.*, Chap. 157 and 361) and, consequently, they are also dispensed from making a pact with the Pole (*quṭb*) (*Fut.*, vol. 3, p. 136).

155. This *ḥadīth* appears in most of the canonical collections and, in particular, in Muslim (*Ṣalāt*, 222), a frequent source of the Amir.

156. This verse is often interpreted in Sufism as a warning against any pretension of attaining the divine Ipseity (see, for example, *Fut.*, vol. 1, p. 271), and not simply as an exhortation to practice the "fear of God." This is clearly the meaning which ʿAbd al-Kader intends here.

157. The "supreme Pleroma" corresponds to the highest degrees of the world of the angelic spirits (*ʿālam al-arwāḥ*).

158. See notes 134 and 136.

159. The "Two Hands"—one which is the Hand of God which gathers the "People of Paradise," and the other which holds the "People of Hell"—are mentioned in a *ḥadīth* reported by Ibn Ḥanbal (4/176 and 323) and by Tirmidhī (*tafsīr*, 2/2).

160. We must clearly read *mushrikīn* and not *mushriʿīn*.

161. This is one of the fundamental theses of the Muʿtazalite school and notably of its founder, Wāṣil b. ʿAṭā (d. 131/748).

162. *Bi-mashiʾati Llāh wa amrihi al-irādī*: these two terms *mashīʾa* and *amr irādī* are equivalent in the Akbarian vocabulary. The *amr irādī* (or *takwīnī*), the divine order by virtue of which things are, is distinct from *amr taklīfī*, "the normative order," which institutes the legal prescriptions. The act "willed" by God in the case of a given creature is not necessarily that which he has prescribed for that creature (Cf. *Fut.*, vol. 3, p. 356; *Fus.*, vol. 1, p. 165).

163. *Awliyāʾihi*: this word can be translated as "his saints." The expression "The saints of Satan" (*awliyāʾ al-shayṭān*)—this inverted "sainthood," which is that of those beings who are the human supports of the infernal powers—is of Koranic origin. (Kor. 4:76)

164. ". . . The tongue of their states" (*bi-alsinati ḥāliha*): this expression applies, for ʿAbd al-Kader as well as for Ibn ʿArabī (*Fus.*, vol. 1, p. 60), to everything which proceeds from a demand that is not formulated but is inscribed in the very nature of the *aʿyān thābita*, in contrast to expressly formulated requests (*al-sūʾāl bi-l-lafẓ*), which the creatures can address to God. Ibn ʿArabī further refines this distinction by discerning, going from the most explicit to the most implicit, three categories of requests: *bi-l-lafẓ*,

"by speech"; *bi-l-ḥāl,* "by state"; *bi-l-istiᶜdād,* "by essential predisposition." The immediate knowledge of the *istiᶜdādāt* is reserved for God, but knowledge of them mediated by means of states (*aḥwāl*) is accessible to the creatures.

165. This refers to the *Ṣaḥīḥ* of Muslim (*imān,* 78).

166. This rule is an application of a more general commandment, that of ordaining the good and prohibiting evil (*al-amr bi-l-maᶜrūf wa l-nahy ᶜani l-munkar*). The words which we translate customarily by "good" (*maᶜrūf*) and "evil" (*munkar*) refer respectively, according to the meaning of their roots ᶜARF and NKR, to notions of "knowledge" and "ignorance" and thus lend themselves to doctrinal developments, a narrowly moral interpretation of which would only touch upon the most contingent aspects. The verb rendered here as "oppose" properly signifies "transform", "change", "alter": this transformation of evil into good, beyond the literal sense (which still retains its full force), is, in its highest form, a "transmutation"—which only metaphysical knowledge can effectuate—which separates that which, in the "evil", is purely negative, therefore illusory, from that which must necessarily be positive in it (without which evil would have no reality whatsoever).

167. Extinction in the divine Unicity abolishes the Law which, being a relation, necessarily implies duality. For the seeker (*murīd*), to see God as Agent of the acts of others is both a necessary condition of spiritual realization and the doctrinal foundation of the most demanding ethic. However, for him to see God as the sole Agent of his own acts—even though this has the same metaphysical basis as the former—runs the risk of leading to antinomianism (*ibāḥa*).

168. Concerning this problem of the "attribution of acts," see texts 32 and 34 and *Fut.*, vol. 2, p. 204; vol. 3, p. 211.

169. The beginning of this verse refers to the order (mentioned in the preceding verse) which Jacob gave to his sons at the time of their second sojourn in Egypt that each should enter by a different gate. The narrative in Genesis does not mention this order but it is reported in certain *Midrashim* (cf. Sidersky, *Les Origines des légendes musulmanes* [Paris, 1933], p. 66–67).

170. The problem of "secondary causes" has given rise in the history of Sufism to debates whose divergences center around the practical consequences to be drawn from the doctrine: Can *faqr*

(spiritual poverty) and *tawakkul* ("trust in God," or better yet, "abandonment to God") be reconciled with having an occupation? Is it better to beg than to earn one's bread? Is it legitimate for the *faqīr* to have recourse to the care of a doctor? The responses of the masters to these questions are extremely varied, but the interpretation of these divergences should take into consideration the concrete situations in which the responses were given and the spiritual state of the disciples to whom they were addressed. Ibn ᶜArabī summarizes—and validates—the two conceivable fundamental positions with respect to "dependence on secondary causes" (*al-iᶜtimād ᶜalā l-asbāb*) in a passage on the symbolism of ritual ablution (*Fut.*, vol. 1, p. 339). He deals with the practical rules which the novice should respect concerning his means of existence in the *Tadbīrāt ilāhiyya* (see the translation of this text in Asin Palacios, *El Islam cristianizado* [Madrid, 1931], p. 363). The theme of this chapter, with reference to the case of the sons of Jacob, is taken up again in text 38.

171. "When they had been unjust toward themselves" (literally: toward their souls): this expression, which is found frequently in the Koran, applies to every being who disobeys the divine orders, since this disobedience causes harm only to themselves and not to God. "They had come to you": "you" designates the Prophet.

172. While *baṣar*, plural *ᶜabṣār*, designates sight in the sensible organs; *baṣīra*, plural *baṣāʾir*, applies, in *taṣawwuf*, to the "inner eye," the organ of suprasensible sight.

173. The first meaning of the root GhFR, from which the verb is derived and which we have translated, according to usage, as "ask pardon" is in fact identical to the meaning of the root STR which means "hide," "veil," "protect." *Istighfār*, asking pardon of God, consists, therefore, from the esoteric point of view, in asking God to "cover," by His acts, His attributes and, finally, by His very Essence, the acts, the attributes and the essence of His creatures. In other words—the process thus described being purely subjective—it consists in dissipating the illusory autonomy of the ego and becoming conscious of that which, metaphysically, has always been. This interpretation of the root GhFR and its derivations is that of Ibn ᶜArabī (see for example *Fus.*, vol. 1, p. 71, 149; *Fut.*, vol. 3, p. 352; vol. 4, p. 145).

174. This "return" of the shadow to its source takes place, in the sensible order, when the sun is at its zenith. It corresponds,

therefore, in the order of metaphysical knowledge, to the moment when the sun of the divine Light shines at the "zenith of being," it being understood that in both cases the movement of the sun is only apparent and that only the earth or the creature moves with respect to it.

175. The esoteric interpretation of the Koran implies that there is no verse and no word which is not susceptible to an application *hic et nunc*. The verse commented upon here, which in its first instance was addressed to contemporaries of the Prophet, should not be taken as having a meaning tied to specific historical circumstances outside of which it would not have full validity. Consequently, the grace which comes from the intercession of the Prophet is as accessible to believers now as it was during his lifetime. This posthumous role of the Prophet is attested to by several *ḥadīth*s. Cf. concerning this point the argument of Taqī al-dīn al-Subkī, *Shifāʾ al-Siqām* (Beirut, 1978), p. 160ff. which responds to the objections of Ibn Taymiyya and his school.

176. This is in fact the first meaning of the root TWB. The interpretation of the Amir is, here again, in conformity with the method of the Shaikh al-Akbar, for whom, for example, *tawba* (repentance) is *rujūʿ* (return) (*Fut.*, vol. 4, p. 127).

177. Ṣadr al-dīn Qūnawī insists on the difference between *maghfira*—which has as a consequence the transformation of evil acts into good acts—and *ʿafw* (a word which can also be translated as "pardon") which has only the effect of *effacing* the evil acts (*Sharḥ al-aḥādith al-nabawiyya,* ms. Shehit Ali 2825, folio 4b).

177bis. A partial translation of this chapter of the *Mawāqif* has been published by Msgr. Teissier in *Etudes arabes,* 47 (Rome, 1974), p. 30–31.

178. The "descent of the Koran upon the saints" is a privilege attached to the quality of "inheritor" (*wirātha*) of the Prophet. Ibn ʿArabī speaks of this in *Fut.*, vol. 2, p. 94; and vol. 4, p. 178.

179. The *Ṣaḥīḥ* of Ibn Ḥibbān (d. 354/965), is one of the last original collections of *ḥadīth*s. The chain of transmission of the cited *ḥadīth* goes back to Ibn Masʿūd.

180. Ibn ʿAbbās, who was born three years before the hegira and died in 68/686, is considered the "*Tarjumān al-Qurān,*" the interpreter par excellence of the Koran. He is responsible for the transmission of numerous *ḥadīth*s.

181. ᶜAlī b. Abī Ṭalīb, fourth Caliph (d. 40/660). A cousin of the Prophet, ᶜAlī became his son-in-law through his marriage to Fāṭima. The expression "People of the House," used in the subsequent phrase and which is of Koranic origin, traditionally designates the family of the Prophet, understood more or less broadly.

182. "Contraction" (*qabḍ*) and "expansion" (*basṭ*) are technical terms frequently employed in the literature of Sufism. According to Jurjānī, *Taᶜrīfāt* (s.v., *qabḍ*), "These are two states which follow when the servant has passed beyond the stage of fear (*khawf*) and hope (*rajāʾ*). 'Contraction' is for the gnostic (*ᶜārif*) what fear is for the novice. The difference between the two is that fear and hope are linked to a future event, desired or feared, while contraction and expansion are linked to something immediately present proceeding from a supranatural inspiration which dominates the heart of the gnostic." See also Ibn ᶜArabī, *Ist.*, definitions 28–29.

183. *Wa mā ramayta* . . . Ibn ᶜArabī often comments on this verse which affirms the individual reality of the person of the Prophet by attributing the throwing to him, while at the same time denying it by identifying it with the divine Reality itself. See among others *Fut.*, vol. 4, p. 41.

184. Concerning the notion of *wajh*, "face," see text 23.

185. To all the preceding considerations we should add that the use of the preposition *fī* ("in") in the verse commented on throughout this chapter ("Verily, you have *in* the Messenger of Allāh an excellent model") takes on a particular meaning which is brought out by the Akbarian prophetology—as it is presented, in particular, in chapter 73 of the *Fut.* (responses to the questionnaire of Tirmidhi) and in the second *Faṣṣ* of the *Fuṣūṣ al-Ḥikam*. According to Ibn ᶜArabī, in fact, every prophet unites in himself sainthood (*walāya*) and prophecy, the latter manifesting itself outwardly while the former represents the innermost aspect of the prophetic person. Since prophethood cannot be acquired (*muktasaba*) and, in addition, it was definitively closed with the coming of Muḥammad, only the interior aspect of the Prophet, that is to say his *walāya*, can, properly speaking, constitute a model for the believers.

186. ᶜAbd al-Qādir al-Jīlī or al-Jilānī: one of the most illustrious masters in the history of Sufism. He was born in 470/1077, and died in 561/1166. The *ṭarīqa qādiriyya* originates with him,

and as previously noted, the Amir ᶜAbd al-Kader, when he was still young, was attached to this *ṭarīqa* through his father.

187. Abū l-Ghayth b. Jamīl, a Sufi from Yemen, died in 651/1253. This saying is generally attributed to Abū Yazīd al-Bisṭāmī.

188. The "scandalous character" of these two sayings derives from the fact that they appear to imply a superiority of the saints over the prophets. The polemic on this theme has often centered around the writings of Ḥakīm Tirmidhī and on the commentaries which Ibn ᶜArabī made on those writings, in particular in his responses to the "questionaire" of Tirmidhī; responses which are found, on the one hand, in an independent treatise, the *Jawāb mustaqīm*, and, on the other hand, in chapter 73 of the *Futūḥāt*. Summarily, we can say that for Ibn ᶜArabī every *nabī* (prophet) is eminently a *walī* (saint) and that *in him* the *walāya* (sainthood) is superior to the *nubuwwa* (prophethood), since the first expresses a permanent spiritual degree while the second corresponds to a limited function in time.

189. Shiblī: a Sufi of Baghdad who was born in 247/861 and died in 334/945. ᶜAbd al-Karim al-Jīlī, in his *Insān Kāmil*, chapter 60 (Cairo, 1949), vol. 2, p. 46, after reporting this conversation between Shibli and his disciple, adds: "The secret of that is the aptitude of the Prophet for taking on all forms . . . When he manifests himself in the form of Shiblī, Shiblī says to his disciple 'Attest that I am the Messenger of Allāh!' Now, the disciple was a man gifted with intuitive unveiling (i.e. he recognized the Messenger of Allāh under the features of Shiblī). Therefore, he responded: 'I attest that you are the Messenger of Allāh.'"

190. This sojourn in Medina took place in 1280/1864 (*Tuḥfa*, p. 702). Having arrived at Medina on 26 Rajab, the Amir ᶜAbd al-Kader was able to obtain as a place of retreat a house which had belonged to Abū Bakr, the first Caliph (or, more likely, it was a house situated on the site of the first Caliph's house). He remained there in solitude for two months.

191. Since these words are from a *ḥadīth*, it should be understood that ᶜAbd al-Kader does not speak them as a citation of the Prophet, but, in the spiritual state in which he finds himself, he takes them as his own since he is at that time totally identified with the Prophet.

192. We correct *li-annī*, since the sense of the phrase obviously requires the negation *lā*.

193. ᶜAbd al-Karīm al-Jīlī (d. 826/1423) is one of the major figures in the school of the Shaikh al-Akbar. We have previously cited his remarks concerning the conversation of Shiblī and his disciple. In the same passage of his book, he says that he himself saw the Prophet at Zabīd, in 796 A.H., under the features of his own master Ismaᶜīl al-Jabartī.

194. Concerning the "saying of Ḥallāj," see note 6. In translating this citation, we have added the word "being" without which the phrase would appear strange to us. But Jīlī said simply: "when someone meets someone . . . ," which is more general and more respectful of the *adab,* when applying it to Ḥallāj who says: *Anā l-Ḥaqq,* "I am God!"

195. *Al-rawḍat al-sharīfa.* This expression designates a space in the Mosque of Medina between the tomb of the Prophet and his pulpit (*minbar*). According to a *ḥadīth,* this space is "one of the gardens of Paradise."

196. The word *fatḥ,* which we translate as "victory," etymologically signifies "opening" and, in the technical vocabulary of the Sufis, it applies clearly to a "spiritual opening" which marks the crossing over into a new stage of realization.

197. The difference between the "general order" and the "particular order" evoked in this paragraph is as follows: every Muslim is subject to the commandment contained in this verse, and for ᶜAbd al-Kader, that is sufficient reason for proclaiming the blessings he has received. But, in addition, we understand that on numerous occasions this verse was "projected" on his heart, as he usually expresses it, and that, consequently, it had taken on for him the character of an injunction which had been personally addressed to him by God. This is a normal consequence of the "descent of the Koran upon the saints" (cf. note 178) in the course of which each word of the sacred Book is received from its very source and thus is received with the newness, the force—*the originality*—of the original Revelation.

198. Muslim, *Ṣaḥīḥ, faḍāʾil,* 140.

199. Ibn ᶜArabī alludes to this *ḥadīth* in the second chapter of the *Fuṣūṣ* (I, p. 63) and comments upon it as follows: "It is not necessary that the perfect should have preeminence in everything and in every degree: for spiritual men, only the preeminence of the degree of knowledge of Allāh needs to be considered."

200. These two terms, which are of Koranic origin, play a fundamental role in sacred cosmology; the Qalam (Kor. 68:1)—

which is a symbol of the first Intellect—inscribes the divine decrees on the "well guarded Tablet" (*al-lawḥ al-maḥfūẓ* Kor. 85:22) which symbolizes the universal Soul.

201. The author does not use the word *muᶜjiza* here, which is reserved exclusively for miracles accomplished by a prophet in order to authenticate his mission. The expression which he employs means literally ". . . that God would interrupt custom for them"—that is to say, interrupt the "natural" order of things. Of course, this "interruption," from the point of view of the akbarian school, corresponds only to the subjective perceptions of the individuals involved, not to that of the Prophet. This would imply, in effect, a permanence of the cosmos which is in contradiction with the doctrine of "perpetual creation" (*khalq jadīd*). Cf. note 32.

202. The author is referring here to the episode of Sura *Yūsuf* already commented upon in text 34. The "participation in prophethood"of Joseph's brothers results from the fact that the "blood of the prophets" flows in their veins. It manifests itself notably in their aptitude—which they possess in common with Joseph—for interpreting dreams. This aptitude is demonstrated by the fear expressed by Jacob in Koran 12:5 when he recommends to Joseph not to describe to his brothers the vision—corresponding to that in Genesis 37:9–10—which he had just confided to his father.

203. Muslim, *Ṣaḥīḥ*, *dhikr*, 41.

204. *Min ḥaythu huwa* and not *hiya* as it appears in the printed text.

205. The *ulūha*, or *ulūhiyya*, which we translate as "function of divinity," designates for Ibn ᶜArabī and his school a degree (*martaba*) of the Essence: that in which the latter is considered, not in itself, that is to say, not as transcending every kind of relation, but insofar as it is worthy of worship, which implies the existence of a worshipper (cf. *Fut.*, vol. 1, p. 42; vol. 3, p. 314). The translation cannot render the force of the Arabic text which utilizes, in this and the subsequent sentence, terms from the same root (*ulūha*, *maᵓlūh*; *maᶜbūd*, *ᶜabd*).

206. These words correspond to modalities of theophanic unveiling, as indicated supra with respect to text 10.

207. Although in other contexts the Name Allāh can represent the Essence in relation to the other divine Names which

represent the attributes and the acts, here it expresses the first determination of the divine Essence which, being absolutely undetermined, is symbolized by the pronoun *huwa*, "He," which in grammar, as we have already remarked, is the "pronoun of the absent person."

208. The author employs here the terms *maʾlūh* and *ilāh*, grammatically correlative, which express in an immediate way for an Arabic reader the logical correlation between what they signify. But as follows from note 205, the disappearance of *ilāh* ("god"), that is to say of the "function of divinity," leaves the divine Essence as such unaffected.

209. The text specifies that this refers to the "second separation" (*al-farq al-thānī*). Concerning this notion see note 57.

210. This *ḥādīth* is in fact commented upon in M. 92 (p. 195 of the Arabic text), in M. 126 (p. 276) and in M. 214 (p. 477).

211. The editor points out—in one of the rare notes which he adds to the text—that this citation of a poem by Imrān b. Hiṭṭān (d. 84/703) contains an error: the first word should be *yawman* and not *ṭawran*. Neither the meter of the verse nor its sense are affected by this lapse of memory. ʿAdnan and Maʿadd are the legendary ancestors of the Arabs of the north, whereas Yemen corresponds to the south of the peninsula.

212. Allusion to a *ḥadīth* (Muslim, *masājid*, 5–8, Bukhārī, *taʿbīr*, 11) which expresses primarily the character of definitive totalization and fulfillment of previous revelations which the mission of the "Seal of the Prophets" has, but it also contains other complementary meanings. For Ibn ʿArabī, the "Sum of Speech" represents also the knowledge of that which is named by the Names which God taught to Adam (*Fus.*, vol. 1, p. 214) or, further, the knowledge of God simultaneously in His transcendence and in His immanence (*Fus.*, vol. 1, p. 71).

213. *Anā ḥaqq*, without the article.

214. This ecstatic song (rhyme in *dāl*, meter *hazaj*), entitled *waḥdat al-wujūd* ("Unicity of Being") by the editor, appears on page 162 of the *Dīwān*.

Index